~ Also by ~
# J.E. WILLIAMS

The Andean Codex:
Adventures and Initiations Among the Peruvian Shamans

Winter Rain
(poetry)

Prolonging Health:
Mastering the 10 Factors of Longevity

Viral Immunity:
A 10-Step Plan to Enhance Your Immunity
Against Viral Disease Using Natural Medicines

Beating the Flu:
The Natural Prescription for Surviving
Pandemic Influenza and Bird Flu

LIGHT of the ANDES

J.E. WILLIAMS

For Kara
Newport Aug 2013
Walk in beauty.
Dance in the light!

LIGHT of the ANDES

In Search of Shamanic Wisdom in Peru "Santiago"

ayniglobal

Copyright © 2012
by J.E. Williams

All rights reserved. Printed in the United States of America. No part of this book may be used or reproduced in any manner without written permission except for brief quotations for review purposes only.

Title image: *North face of Ausangate*
Cover image and interior photographs by J.E. Williams
Cover and interior design: ital art by Mariah Fox
Map by Grupo Geo Graphos S.R.L., Miraflores, Peru

Light of the Andes is published by Irie Books and sponsored by AyniGLOBAL, a non-profit organization dedicated to indigenous wisdom, including producing literature, film, and workshops on the relationship of humans and nature, earth-based wisdom, and optimal personal health of mind and body.

Inquiries, please contact Dr. Williams
Phone: (941) 929-1901
Fax: (941) 929-1903
Email: drjewilliams@gmail.com

ISBN 10: 1-61720-374-2
ISBN 13: 978-1-62720-374-9
First Edition

10 9 8 7 6 5 4 3 2 1

∼

For the coming generations,
who will create a new world.

∼

CONTENTS

Map of Greater Cusco Area x
Author's Note xv
Preface xix
Acknowledgements xxv

Chapter One   Sebastian's Dilemma 3
Chapter Two   The Teaching of Suryamana 25
Chapter Three   The Way to Ausangate 55
Chapter Four   Earth Mountain Sky 83
Chapter Five   White Clouds Green Lake 99
Chapter Six   Blue Transparent 119
Chapter Seven   The Last Mountain 135

Epilogue 149
Sebastian Note 155
Topics for Discussion 156
Notes & References 157
Quechua Glossary 160
About the Author 167
About AyniGLOBAL 169

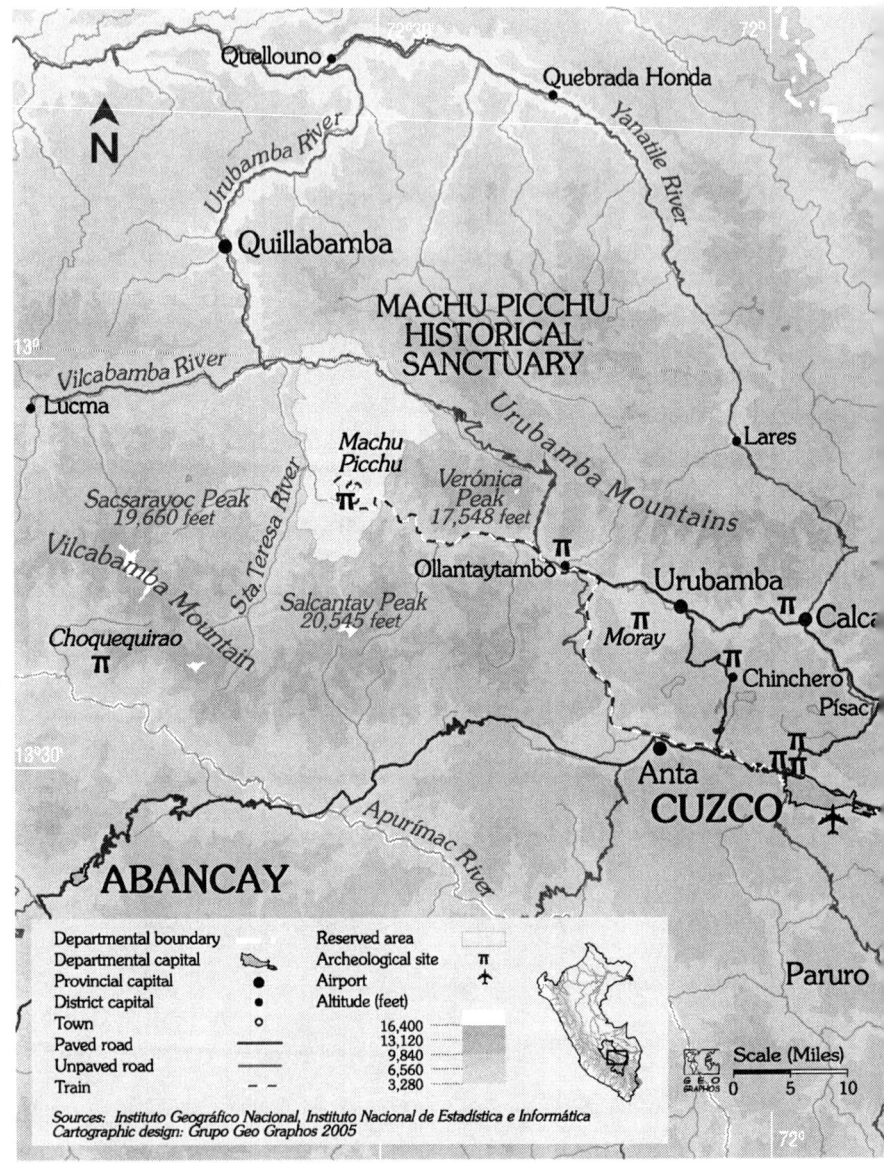

Map of Greater Cusco Area

*Greater Cuzco area from Machu Picchu to
Ausangate Peak, including Q'ero Territory.*

To develop a sense of universal responsibility, of the universal dimension of our every act and of the equal right of all others to happiness and not to suffer, is to develop an attitude of mind whereby, when we see an opportunity to benefit others, we will take it in preference to merely looking after our own narrow interest.

∼ The Dalai Lama

~ Author's Note on ~
QUECHUA TERMS

It is extremely difficult to translate the complex cosmology and ancient spiritual teachings of the Q'ero into English. For one, there are many variations of phonetic Quechua spellings. For example: Cuzco, Cusco, Q'osqo...or Inca, Inka. In this book, I choose accepted spelling for places, like Cusco, and daily items even if different from the dictionary. Another reason is that Quechua is a spoken language, written Quechua being a recent development. In spoken Quechua, single words tend to be linked together, forming sequences that build concepts leading to encompassing philosophical statements of worldview leaving individual words or explanatory sentences inadequate. These multiword constructs are not listed in Quechua dictionaries, yet native speakers understand them with ease. To their ear, the words flow like water over stones, polishing until smooth. In keeping with spoken Quechua, in an attempt to retain their poetic, dreamlike quality, I link words as consistent with common usage.

For consistency in this book, I've used Quechua spellings from the *Diccionario Quechua-Espanol-Quechua* by The Academia Mayor de la Lengua Quechua in Cusco.[1] This dictionary is the same one I used for Quechua terms in *The Andean Codex*. I also include a glossary of Quechua words. However, there are considerable regional variations among Andean Quechua speakers, not all the words and terms used by the Q'ero in this book are found in that dictionary. In fact, many Quechua words in this book are part of an ancient language spoken by the Inkas.

Common Quechua, *Runasimi,* was the language originally spoken in pre-Inkan times by the people of the Andean highland valleys in the Cusco area. The Inkan royalty, who came from outside of the Cusco valley, had their own language that scholars believe was related to Chimu, a now extinct language spoken by a pre-Inkan Peruvian coastal civilization centered around Chan Chan, near the site of the current day city of Trujillo on the Pacific in the north of Peru. After establishing Cusco ("Navel of the World") as the capital city of the Inkan empire, *Tahuantinsuyu* ("Empire of the Four Directions"), the Inkas adopted Quechua as the official language of the empire, but continued to use their private language among themselves and the priestly class. Because the Inkas had no formal written language that we know of, this sacred language is hardly known, though still in use among elder Q'ero shamans.

Many of the words and terms used in this book, as held by the Q'ero, are in the original sacred language of the Inkan royalty, and therefore are not found in any Quechua dictionary. In these cases, I've attempted to come as close to the form of spelling used by the Academia Mayor, and according to Sebastian's wishes, I refer to these ancient terms in this book as "Sacred Runasimi."

Previous page:

Sebastian playing Q'ero flute.

Right: *Santiago and Sebastian in Cusco.*

PREFACE

I never was good at being the invisible witness, the objective ethnographer observing impersonally the lives of human subjects. It did not work for me in 1967 when I lived with the Yupik people of St. Lawrence Island in the Bering Sea, and it does not apply to my work with the Q'ero. In keeping with the legacy of my fieldwork, *The Light of the Andes* is a work of hybrid ethnography and spiritual anthropology about the teachings of *Ayni,* the Q'ero way of knowledge and being. It is not a record of events and things. Rather, it forms a personal narrative, an allegory of seeking and discovery that documents the events that lead to the journey and high-altitude initiation on Ausangate with the traditional Q'ero shaman and wisdom keeper, Sebastian Pauccar Flores, in 2008.

Ayni is the touchstone of the Q'ero worldview who hold it as the code of life, an innate imprint discoverable in nature and ever present in the universe where it forms the content of every thing—the matrix of all being. Ayni is best thought of as reciprocity, but it also implies reverence and universal responsibility. On Earth, it is embedded in nature's design. In the human sphere, it acts as a golden compass that always points true. Neither a religion nor a philosophy, Ayni is the guiding principle for a way of life that embodies ethical behavior and spiritual practice that promotes reverence for the earth and the heavens, family and culture; that fosters social harmony and engenders a common sensibility for all life—the sustainability principle.

Since 2000, I have been a friend to the Q'ero. Living and working with them has brought me to a deeper understanding of nature and myself. Sebastian and I have walked hundreds of miles together in the Andean mountains, long marches at high altitude with few breaks, little water and often no food, and when necessary sleeping in the open without tents or trekking gear. I learned their history, shared their beliefs, and studied Quechua. I listened to their dreams and they listened to mine. I followed their traditional spiritual practices; conducted more than a hundred ceremonies of reciprocity (called *despachos*) with Q'ero shamans *(pakuqs or paqos)*, and have adapted these practices into my daily life. During this time with the Q'ero, babies have been born, children have come of age, young men have fathered children, and good friends have died.

I wrote *The Andean Codex* [2] to document my encounters with Sebastian between 2000 and 2004. In it I presented five underlying principles of human ethical behavior in relationship to each other, community, nature, and the universe as held by the Q'ero—a way of being that we might learn from to make life worthwhile. This book presents deeper insights and teachings from the vantage point directly of a well-respected traditional Q'ero shaman.

In November of 2006, Sebastian and I went to Lima together to promote the book. This was his first time in the Peruvian capital, and the number of cars, throngs of people, and size of buildings surprised and astonished him. However, it was the soul of modern civilization that caused a dilemma of unprecedented consequences for Sebastian—one that was to compel our journey to Ausangate.

In 2007, Sebastian told me that the Apus had informed him that it was time to reveal the Q'ero teachings and ancient shamanic principles in detail. Though a series of visions, insights, and dreams, I embarked on my quest: how to present the deeper meaning of Ayni to the world, and how to present the Q'ero teachings in an authentic manner. Sebastian emphasized that it was his responsibility to pass on an ember of this knowledge just as the cultural fire is going out among his people, and it was my mission to rekindle reverence for life and nature among people in the world at large.

Preface

For more than forty years prior to working with Sebastian, I pursued the elusive secret of the Andes. Now, amazingly, it was revealed; not in a hidden kingdom of immortal spiritual adepts, but alive and well among natives of the Peruvian Andes, the Q'ero.

In 2008, Sebastian and I journeyed to Apu Ausangate, the central Apu of the Inkas and the highest mountain in the entire Cusco region; this was the first time for both of us. The *Apukuna,* the permanently snow-capped peaks, symbolize every thing profound, powerful, inaccessible, and mysterious that lies outside the realm of human comprehension. The white summits of the highest most spectacular mountains are the realm of the Apukuna, the Lords of the Andes. The spiritual ruler of them all is Apu Ausangate.

To the Q'ero, and all traditional, indigenous people of the Andes, the Apukuna are ancient living intelligences—master spiritual teachers. When they are gone, so goes the prophecy, we will forget who we are, where we came from, where we are going. Mostly though, we'll forget how to live harmoniously on this planet according to Pachamama's teaching of Ayni. The sense of the sacred will vanish with the forests and mountains, and a total absence of reverence for nature will allow for no nature. Much of this has already happened in the modern world and we are witnessing it each day.

In this book, you will find that Ayni also takes the form of a spiritual path, which constitutes the essence of the teachings. The Q'ero wish that Ayni, upon which Earth-based indigenous wisdom and heart-centered spirituality rests, may serve as a model for a sustainable future.

In May 2010, I returned to Peru to gather additional details for this book. In the same year, with the encouragement of the Q'ero, I founded AyniGLOBAL, a non-profit organization in Washington, D.C. to support our mission and charitable work in Peru.

In October 2011, I traveled back to Cusco to review the manuscript with Sebastian and other Q'ero of his lineage. This was to assure accuracy. During mountain sojourns, effects of high altitude and cold make note taking difficult. Illegible jottings and single words along with photographs form the record of my

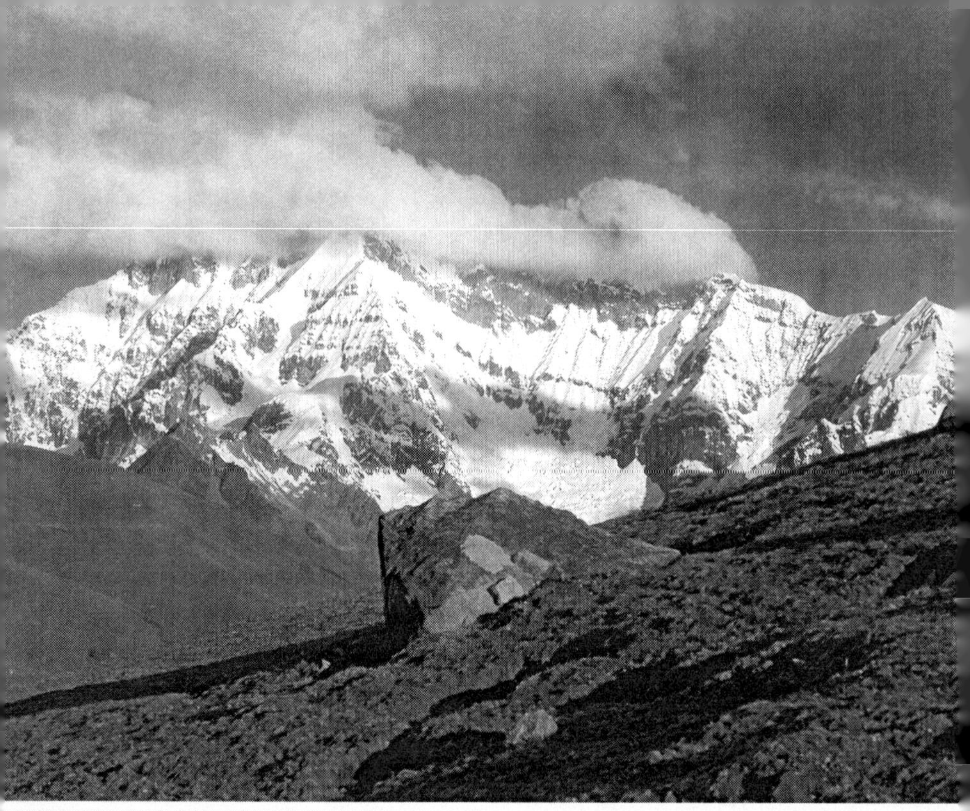

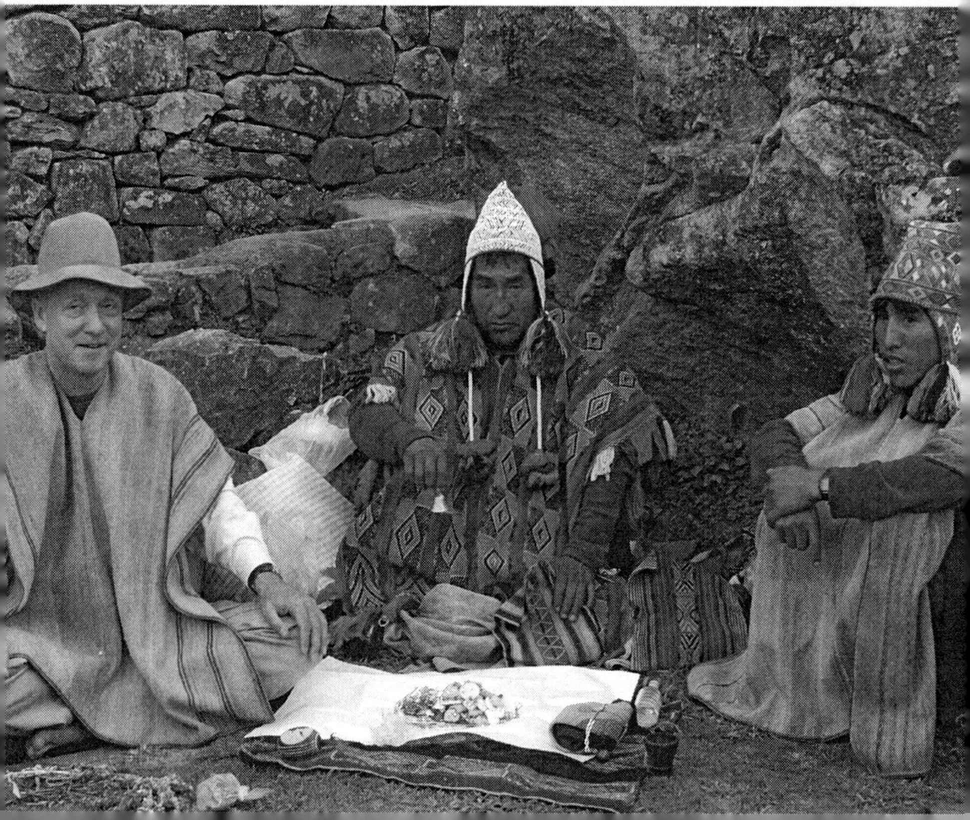

encounters. Later, I recreated them from memory; subsequently we held numerous meetings to clarifying the teachings and fill in the blanks where memory fails.

Throughout the book, I refer to myself using my shamanic name, "Santiago." This was given to me decades earlier in Oaxaca, Mexico. I carried it back to Peru and it stayed with me in the Andes.

~ J. E. Williams (Santiago)
Cusco, Peru
October 2011

Top: *Northeast approach to Ausangate.*

Bottom: *Santiago (left), Sebastian, and Nicolas preparing for the journey to Ausangate.*

ACKNOWLEDGEMENTS

My deep appreciation goes to Sebastian Pauccar Flores, and to all the members of my adopted Q'ero family. Without our special bond, my experiences would not have been as rich. Special thanks go to Nicolas Pauccar Calcina. During the research and writing of this book, we worked closely together on the Quechua to Spanish translations of his father's teachings.

The support of additional Peruvian friends made my work possible. In Lima and Iquitos there was the gracious Chong family. In Cusco, there was Jackeline Bacca Fernandez and her multigenerational family, who housed and fed me, provided friendship and comfort, and insights into Andean life. Thanks go to Julio Camacha who helped with much of the logistical support for my expeditions.

Thanks to my editors, Gerald and Loretta Hausman, who worked with me on *The Andean Codex* and helped pull the manuscript for this book along to its final form. A very heartfelt acknowledgement goes to Marz Attar. Without his advice and support, we could not have made the progress we did in our non-profit work with the Q'ero community. He exemplifies a truly altruistic, spiritual lifestyle.

And to Melvis Hernandez Lara, from Santiago de Cuba, for her patience and understanding during my long absences in Peru while writing my books. Nothing could have been done without the intensity and poetry of her presence.

I am indebted to all of you and countless others along the shamanic way in Peru.

Previous page:
Sebastian praying at Pachacamac.

CHAPTER ONE

SEBASTIAN'S DILEMMA

November 2006

The sky is painted turquoise. Though not the macaw blue of the eastern Andes plunging into green rainforest that Sebastian is familiar with, it is a sky, beautiful and rare for a city blanketed months at a time in a thick inversion layer of gray clouds coming off the Pacific, to mark today as a good day. After a bone-jolting eighteen-hour bus ride over the Andes from Cusco to the arid Pacific coast, Sebastian arrives for the first time in Lima. Dressed in short charcoal-colored alpaca leggings, natural fawn colored poncho, and a bright red and yellow woven cap with white beading, he stands alone on the bus platform. Then, takes his first step on asphalt and concrete. When he sees me, we embrace, our connection strong as ever.

Sebastian is a traditional *pampamisayoq*, a shaman-priest of the Q'ero nation, a *hanpiq* or healer, and a *kukawatoq*, one who divines with coca leaves. He refers to himself as "a servant of the Apus and Pachamama." Born in 1960 into a family of shamans, Sebastian's father, Juan Pauccar Flores, a well-known and beloved pampamisayoq, was a positive influence on his career. But, Sebastian traces his lineage to other shamans from both his mother and father's traditions, crediting his extensive knowledge to his grandfather, the pampamisayoq Andres Espinosa, and an uncle who was an *altomisayoq,* the highest level of Q'ero shaman-priest. However, none of his illustrious background from the remote world of the Q'ero has prepared him for the urban sprawl of Lima.

I am concerned that he might become bewildered by the size of the capital, but I am wrong. Instead of having culture shock, he is enthralled by the tall buildings, the width of avenues, the mass of people, the onrush of so many vehicles. His initial amazement soon fades, and Sebastian becomes deeply concerned by what he sees and experiences. The consequence of this is to create an existential dilemma for him, and an unprecedented challenge for me.

Prior to 2000, few Q'ero, including Sebastian, visited Cusco. They spoke no Spanish and few had contacts among *Cusqueños,* mestizo residents of Cusco. In Lima, a sprawling city of eight million, the Q'ero are virtually unknown. He has never been this far from his beloved *Apus.*

In the Andes, he is immune to physical hardship, cold, and hunger; no burden is too heavy and no distance too far. Though completely at home in the wilderness, he is an alien in Lima. It is not the urban topography that unsettles him or that *Limeños,* Peruvians of European-Creole decent, are different from the indigenous Andean people he is accustomed to, it is the nature of humanity itself that first arouses his curiosity and then pushes him toward a state of unease that disrupts his native equilibrium. In this sprawl of dust clinging to the Pacific jammed with people tearing madly about in dilapidated taxis and overcrowded minivans, it is the sense of isolation that unnerves him. The collision of mass humanity strikes a discordant note with his personal values. Here the barrage of personalities, the relentless rush of people in pursuit of material happiness is disconcerting for me, let alone Sebastian. For him though—just for the moment—it is exhilarating. He doesn't yet know how debilitating it can be. He doesn't understand the machinations of such a vast and improbable city. When he does, it will appear to him as madness.

Chapter One: Sebastian's Dilemma

~

We take a taxi from the bus station. Sebastian is quiet on the forty-minute ride to the other side of the city, but as he steps out of the cab, he exclaims *"hatun hoteles"* at the many tall building that line the streets. I inform him they are not "big hotels," but apartment buildings, explaining that they are urban high-rise dwellings that house several hundred people.

He is not convinced, and over the next several days makes a game of it, but for the moment I suggest we walk for a few blocks to orient him to the neighborhood before settling into our lodging.

The three-story apartment building where I live in Miraflores, a well-kept residential district of Lima, is three blocks from the Pacific. Sidewalks are planted with trees, and parks are tidy. Cafes and restaurants line the main streets, and it is considerably less crowded than other parts of Lima. The apartment building, a concrete and brick rectangle with long windows lining the outer rooms is simple and functional. Planted with shrubs and flowering plants that form the inner-gated entry makes for a simple, but welcome urban oasis. Trees line the street in front, where gentle Pacific Doves[3] with blue halos around their eyes perch just outside my windows cooing before nightfall and every morning, softly welcoming the day.

"This one *must* be a hotel," he says, pointing at a high-rise on the same block.

"No, that's another apartment," I counter.

We round the corner and come to Jose Pardo Avenue, both sides lined with even taller business buildings and executive hotels. A tree lined park runs for ten blocks up the middle, and we stroll along, pausing from time to time as he turns three sixty so not to miss a thing. For a while, we sit on one of the benches so he can take in people and cars, buildings, and movement of things along the avenue.

As we get closer to Parque Kennedy, one of two main plazas in Miraflores, the buildings get bigger and taller. Sebastian strains his neck backward to look up a vertical wall of glass, and says quietly as if to himself, "More people live in one building than in all of Q'ero."

He stands there, neck craned back, looking up, unblinking, face full of wonderment.

A small, solid man with reddish brown sun-darkened, chestnut-colored skin, Sebastian stands on the corner of the busy city street wearing traditional Q'ero short charcoal alpaca pants and black tunic, the *unku,* hand woven by his wife, Filipa, from the wool sheered from his own alpacas, over which he wears a natural-colored beige poncho and on his head a multicolored knitted cap called a *ch'ulhu,* intricately beaded with designs representing *Inti,* the sun. For footwear, he wears the common sandals of all Andean natives. There is no getting him into shoes, even if city decorum calls for it. He told me once that he tried shoes but his feet hurt so much, he threw them off. He likes to feel the ground through soft flexible sandals, even if here it is concrete, not clumsy bad fitting pieces of hard leather. He now informs me that he will wear the same outfit, including sandals, throughout his visit in Lima.

Because I have lived much of my life among indigenous people, I understand what he is seeing and feeling. A traditional Q'ero individual may meet a few thousand people over a lifetime. Today, within the radius of our ten-minute walk, he is among several hundred thousand people. In his part of the world, people live horizontally, close to the earth. Here, life is vertical. But, it is not just the number of people and the size of buildings that overwhelms him in Lima. It is the proximity of strangers. The intimate bond of familiarity, the inseparability of community creates a social network for Sebastian. It is all one. Here it is all *for* one; there is a vast difference.

I weave him through side streets out of the way of people and cars. He becomes thoughtful. I imagine, seeing all this for the first time, he is concerned for the fate of his people. They are so few; this one city contains so many.

He queries as we walk: "How many cities like this are in the world? Do other countries have cities like Lima? What about the United States? Are there cities as big as Lima? Are there Apus and rivers and lakes and alpaca? Is there any nature left?"

Chapter One: Sebastian's Dilemma

We walk across the park. The grass and trees are a refreshing break from concrete and steel. Women with children, students dressed in navy blue school uniforms, and businessmen in dark suits, halt in their hurried pace to stare, open-mouthed, at Sebastian. He takes no notice. I change course to avoid gawkers and weave us through less crowded corners of the park to a quiet restaurant where locals dine and where we will not be disturbed.

We have lunch of grilled fish and eat *papa a la huancaína,* a traditional Peruvian dish of sliced boiled potatoes covered in a spicy yellow cream sauce accompanied with boiled eggs and burgundy colored wine-cured olives. He is thankful, but not impressed with the food, preferring simpler and more abundant fare like roasted potatoes and whole trout fried in llama fat.

As a rule, Peruvians are polite, and there is no finger pointing or yelling, or children running up to touch him, but when we finish and I lead him across the park on our way back to my apartment, people stop and stare. Even small dogs watch attentively, but they do not bark.

He appears not to notice, instead commenting on the beautiful trees, thick trunked and fully leaved, but I decide he needs a break, so hail a taxi to take us to Malecon Luis Cisneros, a well kept green belt above the Pacific that provides an unobstructed view of sleek gray water reaching to the horizon. Several hundred feet below the bluffs, the crash of surf echoes off sandstone walls.

"How big is the world," he wants to know, as he looks out over the ocean.

I put my own concerns aside, and turning to the ocean join him in the silence of friendship that knows no boundaries.

"The world is immense and diverse with great seas and majestic mountain ranges, and filled with billions of people," I answer. "There are many cities bigger then Lima."

He wants to know how many and which ones are the biggest.

I have no idea exactly how many megacities the planet supports, and tell him that there are at least twenty with over ten million people and at least a hundred big cities like Lima, maybe more. I count off some: "In Latin American there is Rio de Janeiro, Sao Paolo, and Mexico City, and there are others like Beijing in China, and Cairo in Egypt, and Karachi in Pakistan. In Europe there is Paris and London, and in America we have New York and Los Angeles, and many very big cities like Boston, San Francisco, and Miami."

He looks at me blankly, as if I said something that made no sense; that did not register in any of his personal or ancestral memories, but only existed in abstraction, beyond grasp of what he knew as real, as if I were making the numbers up, a pure fiction.

He wants to know about "nature" in other countries. I explain that there are different animals than in Peru and that alpaca and llamas are unique to the Andes, existing in their native state as *vicuñas*[4] only in Peru and Bolivia. I go on about the great snowcapped mountains, powerful wise Apus in Tibet and Nepal, and of amazing mountains in China and India and Pakistan, how thousands circle Mount Kailas, the greatest Apu of the Himalayas—a holy mountain in western Tibet sacred to Buddhism, Hinduism, Jainism, and the shamanic religion of Bon-po. I say that the United States has beautiful Apus, holy places to Native Americans.

Sadly, I admit that there are far fewer wild places, considerably less animals and fish, and the snowcaps on these great Apus are melting fast like they are in the Andes.

"Santiago, the Apus are dying," he whispers, not taking his eyes off the horizon.

~

A dense fogbank has set in, and the sun, hiding behind the gray, not to be ignored, issues refracted light. The low hanging clouds almost touch our heads in an ethereal lavender mist.

We find a bench to sit on and wait for sunset. Our conversation drifts along one sentence at a time, with long pauses between, and after about an hour, as if he heard enough, Sebastian composes himself, sits upright and expectant, as I have seen him before climbing a high pass, preparing for breathlessness.

"There is much to do. It is not only Q'ero and Cusco that are in danger, but from what you tell me, the world is troubled." He states this in his minimalist way of speaking, perhaps for my benefit, more likely because it is his personal style—few words, large impact.

From years of working with Sebastian, I expect him to say little, or nothing at all, allowing the experience to provide its own way of understanding. We will have plenty of time to discuss solutions later as the problem is not going away; for now, I have no answers, so I turn my attention to making his first visit to Lima meaningful and memorable.

Our walk along the *malecon* is his first view of the Pacific; later at the beach, he has his first feel and taste of salt water. It is also his first time staying in a hotel, or rather a small family run hostel, four blocks from where I live. I share my small apartment with friends and there is no room for another person, but Sebastian doesn't mind. A private room is like a suite to him.

It is a good choice, because adjacent to the small room I rent for him on the third floor, there is an outdoor patio tiled with colonial red clay, and every morning and evening for the two weeks that we are in the city together, we start and end our day watching fog build then ebb along the crescent shaped bay that forms the coastline south of Lima. In the last hour of the day, opaque dark walls obscure the horizon; the intersection of sky and ocean blend, and as the fog bank moves towards the shore, all becomes twilight gray.

Because Sebastian prefers to walk rather than take a taxi, we are always around pedestrians. Everywhere we go people marvel. He hardly notices, but I am acutely aware of the sensation he creates. As we walk the well-kept sidewalks of Miraflores and San Isidro, urban Peruvians stare unabashedly and many text message or frantically dial cell phones to tell others what they see. Some stop and stare, unapologetically. Cars circle back, some going around the block several times, while driver and passengers take pictures with cell phones, put their children on the side of the car near us to best see him, small faces pushed against the widows, brown eyes wide as saucers.

~

On the morning of his third day, we head to the business district of Miraflores and walk along Benavides Avenue to a nine-story office building to meet with Maria Luisa, the cartographer who made the beautiful maps for *The Andean Codex,* and where Sebastian has his first elevator ride.

Though not claustrophobic and eager as ever to give something new a try, he questions the purpose of the elevator. I explain that it is a mechanical lift so we don't have to use the stairs. He tells me that legs are meant to climb mountains, or stairs. However, he is game, and the doorman, whose curiosity arouses when Sebastian breaks into Quechua, politely shows us the elevator and then discreetly asks if Sebastian can speak Spanish. "Where is he from?" he asks with incredulity. When I tell him that Sebastian lives in a remote region of Paucartambo near Cusco and speaks Quechua, the doorman looks surprised, and as the elevator door slides open, he politely holds it for us as if we were special guests.

I invite Sebastian to step in, but he steps out immediately.

"It didn't go anywhere," Sebastian says while scrutinizing the elevator. "Are you sure it works?"

"Hai!" I answer and chide him, "You are quickly becoming like an impatient city person. It's a stubborn elevator and takes its time getting going like an old horse."

He steps back in beside me while the doorman presses the seventh floor button and steps out, and up we go—the cable creaking and cracking. Nearing our floor, the elevator jerks up and down before settling to a stop, and as the door opens, Sebastian steps briskly out ahead of me.

Looking around, he says: "Everything is the same as before."

Had we gone anywhere after all, he wonders? The uniform construction of modern commercial buildings puzzles him, and for a moment he cannot believe we have gone up at all until I guide him down the hall and we enter the tiny office of the cartographer.

Maria Luisa, a professional, thoughtful woman of about forty-five is expecting us. More knowledgeable than most in Lima about Andean indigenous culture and its people, she does not stare and invites us to sit at a small table in front of a closed window whose glass is tinted with street grim. The view is compelling: on all sides there are buildings, most taller, pressed together forming walls of glass, concrete, and steel. Below, the sound of traffic and the muffled noise of people funnel upward.

As a man of high mountains, Sebastian is at home with heights and finds the wall of buildings and the distant street below fascinating. Maria Luisa notices his interest and asks, "Would you like a better view?" She reaches across the table where we are seated, and slides open the window. There is a blast of air. Sebastian moves as smooth as a cat, and in one motion, steps on the table and plants his foot on the ledge. As he steps forward, I reflexively grab his poncho tightly to stabilize him without throwing him off balance, my other hand gripping the edge of the table.

Maria Luisa, steps back; gasps. Her hand goes to her mouth, but she doesn't utter a sound. Her pupils, like ink blots, are dilating fast.

"*Papa,*" I whisper, "It is not meant for you to go out on the ledge to look. Please come back in."

He turns with questioning eyes, and then says to me, "What a shame, it looks so beautiful and the air is strong. For a moment, I felt at home."

With white knuckles, I grip his poncho while Maria Luisa's staff of three, having watched from the doorway of the opposite room where they do their cartography work, quickly come to help stabilize the table. Sebastian, pausing for a few more seconds, reluctantly steps back onto the table and takes his seat as if nothing out of the ordinary had happened. Then he closes his eyes and falls asleep sitting up while I continue with the meeting.

~

After several more days of business, I decide we need to get out of the city, so hire a taxi to take us to the archeological site of *Pachacamac*.[5] The place has been in ruins for centuries, but since 2003 restoration has been slowly taking place by a joint effort of Peruvian and American archeologists supported by grants from the

National Science Foundation and the National Geographic Society.

Though the Pachacamac complex is not directly a part of the Q'ero worldview—theirs predates the Inkas and is nestled in the region around Apus Ausangate and Q'ollqepunku—Sebastian is at home among these ruins.

Less than an hour south of Lima in the Lurin River Valley overlooking the Pacific, is a once massive ceremonial complex including the ruins of a pyramid to the sun and the temple of Pachacamac, the oracle of the Inkas considered a direct line of communication to that which animates the world—*Pacha,* the wholeness of life. All that ever existed and will exist, and everything that could or would exist, or not exist is the realm of Pacha. And, *Kamaq* (or "camac" when used for the archeological site, but spelled "Kamaq" when referring to the creator) is the term for the creator of the universe.

In the Q'ero cosmovision, Pacha is composed of three spheres synergistically interacting to form the full spectrum of human experience. Every thing is interconnected from the smallest to the cosmic, and all three spheres are guided by one universal principle—Ayni. Though each has its own unique characteristics, these three spheres are inseparable: ebbing and flowing, merging into each other, ever changing, overlapping, interpenetrating, and interrelated. *Pachakamaq* is the sphere of spiritual life; *Pachamama* of material life, the living world of this Earth; and *Pachakamacha* refers to the social life of humans.

Ever-present, Pachakamaq is the spiritual invisible interpenetrating presence of life. According to the Q'ero, because Pachakamaq exists, we can gain perspective from the past and divine the future. A vast temple complex, including a walled city with gold covered pyramids over looking the Pacific, and an exquisitely designed maze of buildings forming an intricate temple complex for women initiates, *Acllahuasi,* and a painted temple that housed a master shrine where the Inka communicated with the creator of time, space, and earth: Pachacamac was, and still is, a place to know past and future.

To the west of the main shrine, rising from ruble the color of sand, looms the remains of the solar pyramid, the central ceremonial complex. We leave our taxi driver to wait, and walk up a sixty-degree incline and then weave through narrow adobe passages toward the platform at the summit of the crumbling pyramid. As we edge our way upward to meet the noonday sun, a fine powder of dust swirls around each footstep.

We meet a lone watchman, who agrees that we can pray and make a simple offering, but he reminds us that no fires are allowed. Sebastian strides ahead of me at a pace hard to keep up with until he finds a secluded passage that opens to the west in the solar temple that he deigns acceptable for a simple ceremony.

It is approaching noon and there are no shadows. The adobe walls provide some shade, but as the sun reaches it's zenith, the day turns hot—November is late spring in Peru—there is no escape from the solar blaze and the heat becomes unbearable. Sebastian seems not to notice, though he removes his knitted cap, his black hair glistening. He prepares for a mid-day ceremony to Inti, the life-sustaining sun. Ceremonies to Inti are at sunrise or high noon, and those to *Killa,* the moon, are performed at night.

Sebastian and I, shoulders almost touching, kneel together in a powder composed of sand and centuries of crumbled adobe. We face west towards the ocean, with our *misas,* ceremonial bundles containing sacred stones, open on the ground in front of us. We close our eyes, wait. There is nothing but the sound of wind funneling through the passages. A fine grit blows against my skin and seeps under my collar and into my hair. The sun burns hard on my face making my skin feel strangely metallic.

After the meditation, I see that his hair is powdered with reddish dust, and assume mine looks the same. Taking up our misas, we align ourselves to one purpose: the protection of all life. We devote every breath in service to Pachamama, and recommit to walk the path of Ayni with integrity, surrounded by beauty until the end of our days.

I spread an *uncuño,* the hand-woven cloth made from natural alpaca wool formed of four equal squares—white, black, beige, and brown—that Q'ero shamans dedicate for working with coca leaves, directly on the ground in front of us. Taking the bag of coca leaves Sebastian brought with him from Cusco, I pour out a green pile in the center of the uncuño, and we shift through them looking for perfectly shaped leaves. Then taking up clusters of three coca leaves between thumb and forefinger, offer *k'intus* to each other, a ritual sharing of coca leaves made sacred by our intention, and infusing them with our breath, we perform the *phukuyr'tti*. This ritual blowing, breath mingled with air, is a performance of reverence representing a very personal act of Ayni, reciprocity between humans and the Apus, and in this way we offer prayers to the Apus and Pachamama for a good year, for health and harmony of all beings.

Sebastian stands, faces west, and looking up toward the sky, the white sun directly overhead, prays in a loud voice, offering more coca leaves, petitions the blessing of Pachakamaq.

The ceremony is brief but complete, and we gather our things and tidy the site where we sat, leaving no trace, not even a footprint in the powder beneath our feet. Then we slowly head down from the pyramid, back the same way we came through the labyrinth of red sand colored walls. The taxi is waiting and takes us along the same single lane country road, but then loops around the pyramid to the north, and there the ocean opens in front of us.

~

Immediately to the west of Pachacamac is a long sandy beach almost level to the land around it where the Pacific spreads vast and graphite gray. Only a few bone-dry islands interrupt the horizon. When we arrive at the beach, Sebastian wastes no time, walks right in to the water, standing knee deep as gentle waves wash against his legs. Never having been to salt water before, the immensity of the ocean touches him as much if not more then the multi-storied apartments and commercial buildings did upon his arrival to Lima. Watching from the beach, I allow him personal time with the waves, and then join him in the ocean, the water cool on my feet and ankles. In offering to *Qochamama,* the great mother sea, I lay three perfectly shaped coca leaves upon the water and watch them drift in the ebb and flow of the waves until they kiss the shore.

For the remainder of the afternoon, we linger along the beach and take cover from the intense sun under the shade in a grove of trees nearby where a stream flows and quietly enters the sea. It is green and cool in contrast to the desert all around us. We speak little, letting the wind in the trees and the sound of the waves do the talking. My lesson is to listen to the teaching of nature, allowing the experience to integrate with my spirit. As the sun nears the horizon, we drive back to Lima, a silence resting between us, and Sebastian lays his head on my shoulder and falls into a deep sleep.

∼

Over the next week, I introduce Sebastian to more of my acquaintances. Most are academics and business people, though some are students and workers. When meeting him for the first time, they greet Sebastian with as much disbelief as those on the street. There are some awkward moments too. Some ignore him as if they were seeing things. Peruvians, mystical by nature, often see and dream spirits. The apparitions of deceased relatives are not uncommon. So, they develop the habit, call it a form of cultural denial, of ignoring apparitions or visions, knowing that they will disappear if not paid attention. Peru is a culture where real and unreal overlap, distant past and present merge, and both the living and the dead influence the future.

When they find that he is from a forgotten wilderness near Cusco and that Sebastian is an authentic Q'ero shaman with skills of coca leaf divination, invariably each person requests a reading.

Sebastian's procedure is the same for coca leaf readings in Cusco. He and I (as interpreter) find a private corner or separate room where, with the patient present, he spreads out coca leaves on an uncuño, the hand woven cloth used for sharing coca leaves. He then shifts them randomly until certain leaves separate themselves from the rest. This procedure is repeated several times accompanied by ancient prayers to the spirit of the coca plant, called *uramama,* in sacred runasimi. He then calls his spiritual mentors, favored Apus with an affinity for divination. He puts aside leaves that fall separately and repeats the process until there are no more leaves falling from the main bunch. He then separates and isolates all the leaves used for divination, and analyzes each in detail, commenting on each one's unique characteristics, and interprets the signs and marks revealed by the shape of each leaf.

His diagnosis of individual after individual, case upon case is invariably the same: *"El susto,"* he announces in his hard-to-understand, broken Spanish, shaking his head at the dire diagnosis. In his assessment, each of our patients has lost their soul.

To Sebastian, soul loss is real and calling it back and re-integrating soul, mind, and body a requirement for wholeness and healing. A form of mental and emotional illness due to spiritual imbalance, El susto is a well-known condition in Latin America. It goes by different names depending on the vernacular of the country and region, but is most commonly known in Spanish as el susto—soul loss, *la pérdida del alma.*

El susto originates from an unusually strong, or strange encounter with dangerous animals, for example: a jaguar or poisonous serpent. Supernatural entities such as ghosts, saints, shamanic beings, or even magical inanimate objects used by sorcerers can be the cause of this condition. It can also happen after a fall from a high precipice or near drowning. In fact, any dramatic incident or traumatic accident can shake the soul from the body resulting in fragmentation of consciousness. The aftermath of such physical or psychological trauma causes symptoms associated with emotional instability, physical debility, fatigue and exhaustion, and a variety of other morbid symptoms requiring immediate and intensive attention by an experienced *curandero* or shaman.

Traditional therapies for the treatment of el susto include cleansing rituals called *limpiesas,* involving floral baths, scented water and perfumes; brushing the body with plants and herbs or with an egg, massage with scented oils, and shamanic ceremonies some of which involve hallucinogenic plants. Special herbal preparations may be administered as teas or enemas to purge the intestines. Sorcerers use powerful crystals or wooden staves carved into shapes of animals in rituals to protect them during soul retrieval. In Peru, sessions using Ayahuasca or San Pedro, respected and feared shamanic plants with powerful hallucinogenic properties, may be employed. Treatment often lasts through the night, but it can go on for days or even weeks until the soul is returned to the body and the patient cured.

El susto is also found among immigrant populations from Latin America in the United States. In the border region of California and Mexico, I worked with *curanderas* who treated el susto among illegal migrants. The trauma of treacherous border crossings, the wrenching apart of families, and the fear of deportation create deep anxiety resulting in debility, insomnia, unexplained chronic pain, and apathy.

Among indigenous people, it is thought that nature spirits and ghosts of deceased people, as well as negative power spots in nature including unusual formations along a river, in canyons, caves, and springs are easy places to capture souls. In the Amazon, strangely shaped trees are thought to harbor entities capable of causing soul loss. It may also occur during visionary experiences under the influence of natural hallucinogens like Ayahuasca, and especially if an experienced shaman is not present.

What we encounter, and which surprises him because it is different from the form of el susto that he is accustomed to, is a chronic state of soul loss among urban mestizos in Lima. This I believe will also be prevalent among stressed-out people from countries all over the modern world.

The treatment for this form of el susto, Sebastian informs me, will be lengthy and the outcome hopeful at best, and only if applied consistently over time. It is not a matter of simple soul retrieval or a ritual for calling the soul back into the body. A tribal person who, supported by community and nourished in nature, finds the return to balance through rituals and chanting, offerings, and fasting. There is no precedent for modern urban people to regain balance, to restore their soul. Because this new form of soul loss results in a fundamental fragmentation of body mind spirit, caused by the complete separation from Pachamama, it requires comprehensive immersion therapy: reconnecting with nature and personal transformation over time.

"How much time?" I ask.

"Months, years, perhaps a lifetime," he answers, and then pauses.

The sounds of the city—cars and people, buses and construction equipment—drone around us. He turns to me with an intensity I've come to know when he has something of importance on his mind. His obsidian eyes reflect the late afternoon sky, orange bordering on gold.

My mind still, our hearts are one.

"Perhaps never," he says, and turns away.

~

I agree with his diagnosis. The world is in trouble and there is no easy answer. In fact, it is a crisis of such proportions that there is concern for the survival of the planet and life as we know it.

When with Sebastian, I suspend my scientific mind. But it creeps in. As a clinician, I wonder is el susto equivalent to depression? It's a tough question. This condition is not a simple case of the blahs or low mood. It's a kind of cataclysmic dejection lasting weeks, or months, or longer. Like a seriously depressed person who feels hopeless, worthless, and despairing; who is fatigued beyond comprehension, el susto shatters normalcy, upends family life and occupation, and tears through reason, flat lining any sense of pleasure. I know that statistically, nearly a million despairing people take their own lives every year. That's a lot. In industrialized societies and modernizing developing worlds, despite a flood of antidepressant drugs, the number of depressed people is rising. But, it's too simple a connection. I sense something far deeper is at work.

Like any ethical physician, Sebastian cautions that this particular form of el susto is atypical. Rather than induced by sudden shock, it has come on gradually, insidiously, and after years of incubation is now at an advanced stage.

Chapter One: Sebastian's Dilemma

There is no cure, he advises. "But," he says compassionately, "There might be some hope." However, Sebastian informs me, the treatment is both complicated and protracted, and the process of recovery would be slow. I learn from him that each patient we see is in the unenviable state that only many *despachos,* ceremonies of reciprocity, and living in community close to nature can remedy. And even with hope for improvement, the prognosis is very poor.

"Santiago," he states, "We have to do something."

How can one fix the unfixable? Cure the incurable? Like the Mother Goose nursery rhyme, if all the King's men couldn't put Humpy Dumpty back together again, who can? But if left untreated, or ineffectively treated, the disease may worsen. As a result, the problems faced by individuals and society, as well as all living things, will worsen. The planet itself, the sustaining earth, will weaken—and we have seen this already at the beginning of the twenty-first century.

This is the window I need into how Sebastian views the modern world. His analysis is the second opinion that confirms my own. The unstable contemporary world has reached an ethical tipping point. Our scientific arrogance and religious dogmas contribute to fragmentation of consciousness. Deep personality disorders are the results for which there is no easy solution. Fragmentation on such an unimaginable level generates personality disorder and through these cracks the souls of people are escaping by the millions.

We are two planetary physicians pondering the consequences of an epidemic of a chronic spiritual disease, a personality disorder that has no cure, and that most people are unaware. Like the patient in absolute denial that anything is wrong even though laboratory tests show otherwise and who, when reaching the outer limits of denial, is diagnosed with stage four metastatic cancer, becomes desperate for a quick cure at the eleventh hour.

Sebastian's dilemma is clear to him, and me, though he doesn't speak of it in this way. To him, the world is full of rich crazy people living in big boxes driving dazzling pieces of metal. Individual will and ego are in disharmony with natural principles. Society is out of balance with Pachamama. There is an epidemic of disconnection between heart and mind; the soul of humanity seems to have left its collective body. What Sebastian wants to do is find a way for his people to continue in a sea of disruptive change without becoming adrift among the masses who know nothing of the way of Ayni. He also wants to help the unaware return to harmony though a greater awareness of Pachamama.

I share his concerns, and am overwhelmed with my own questions. How can we create a better world, a more equitable society without a guiding principle? Is going forward technologically, but not spiritually, a greater problem than society at large wants to face? Would it rather continue to accept material rewards granted by technology, and thus forget about a saner, healthier way of living? Is the fate of the last few remaining authentic indigenous groups on the planet contingent to our future? Is the Q'ero message going to be lost in exploding population and expanding poverty? Is capitalism, and its stepchild, rampant consumerism going to devour our natural resources without thought of future generations? If these questions are valid, then what of our largest concern—how to cure the world?

Sebastian's dilemma becomes my personal challenge. As a doctor, more than ever, I recognize that we need deep transformational healing. We need a wiser understanding of our relationship with each other and nature...but how can we accomplish this? How are we to make countless fragments whole again? And, I become acutely concerned that it might be contagious. Will it affect Sebastian?

His concern for his people is a microcosm of my concerns for the planet. His interest in cultural survival is an example of the concern we all should have in the wellbeing of others and the continuance of civilization. His sense of ecological responsibility and willingness to act with determination in the face of environmental change is an example of the concern we should have for the global environment. His love for Pachamama is the motivating force we need to employ so that we bond more deeply with our Earth.

The Q'ero describe the world as a seamless interconnection between Pachamama and our body, and between the intelligence of the Apus and our mind. Nature, wilderness, clean water, living oceans, old growth forests with ancient trees are absolutely vital to our human heart, mind, and soul.

"*Compadre,* we have to find a solution," Sebastian looks at me, his eyes narrow like deep canyons, "The world may not be ready to hear our message, but we must try."

I want to believe that we can make a difference. I know that underlying passionate intention is as necessary as quiet sincerity, and that kindness is more important than morality, that good actions tell more about a person than claims to beliefs. I tell my self that there is no harm in trying, and remind myself that we must never put a theory, even one as universal as the light of the Andes, before a human being.

Before we become old men who remember what they could have done, we must try. He says we can influence the trajectory of things. Before civilization reaches the abyss, he wants his people, and all of us, to find salvation. Stopping at the edge before going over will be enough, he thinks. We harden to the task, knowing it will be difficult. We are determined not to grow nostalgic or filled with regret—not to become old men who refused the challenge, the fight, the battle on the edge.

I know only one thing. Sebastian's dilemma has slipped inside me and will not just drift there, but will take hold of my imagination.

We step out on to the street, walk on in silence, cars and people swirl around us.

Sebastian stops, looks to the sky and then at me. "It is time we went to Apu Ausangate for your next initiation. When the Apu calls, we will go."

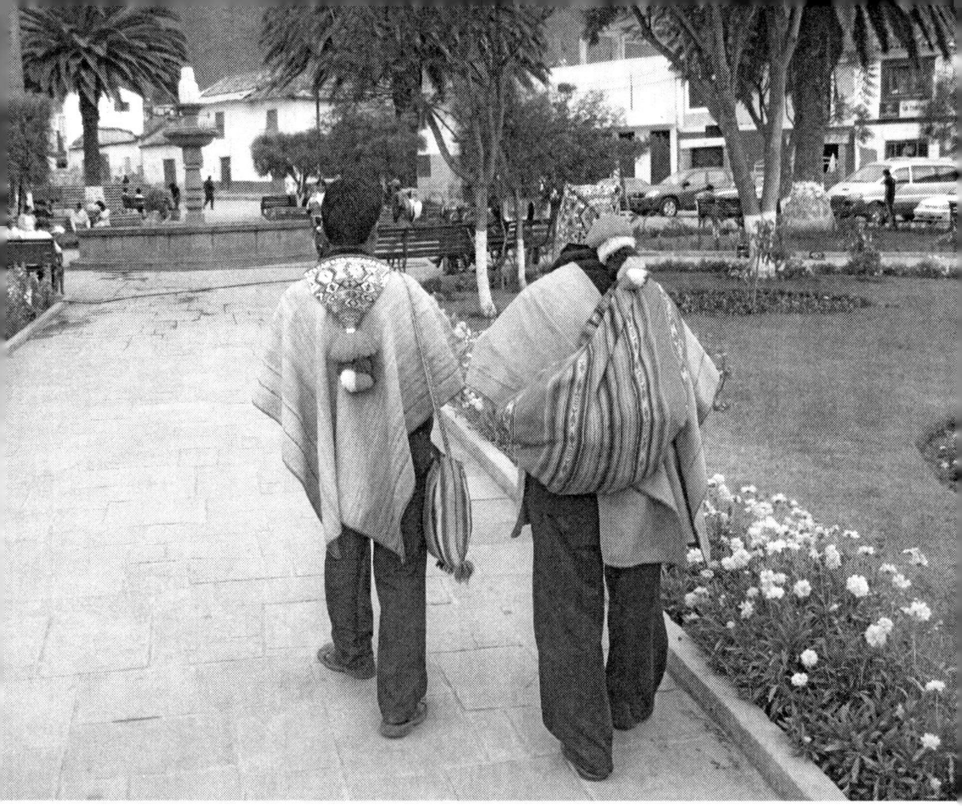

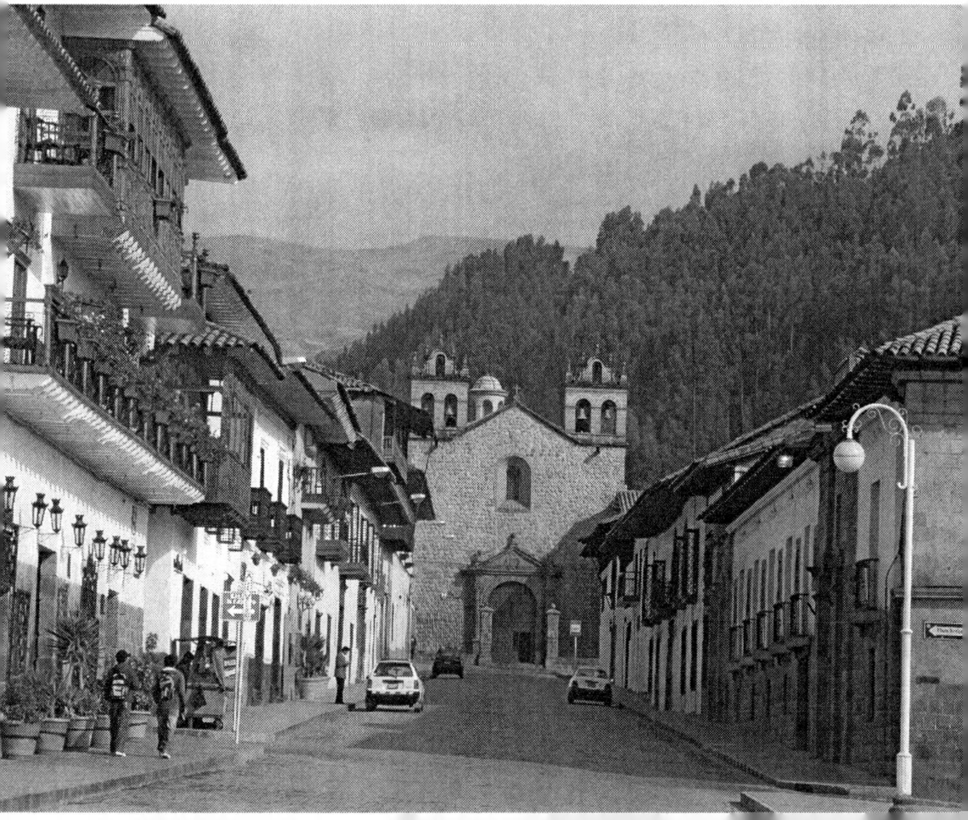

Previous page:

Above: Nicolas (left) and Sebastian in Urubamba.

Below: Calle Heladoeres in Cusco.

~ CHAPTER TWO ~

THE TEACHING OF SURYAMANA

May 2007

Among the Q'ero, dreams are integral to the fabric of life. However, separating the subconscious from the conscious mind would seem arbitrary and fragmented to them. Dreams are to be listened to and followed; not interpreted. In their world, dreams are part of the seamlessness of being. Alive, meant to be lived in the same way clouds move across the sky, or as a trout swims in a clear stream effortlessly in the current, dreams are as real as rising for breakfast.

To the Q'ero, events and things, including dreams, are birthed in their own time, proceed in their own way, and exhibit a timing of their own.

Each morning before the labor of the day begins—preparing soil for planting, shepherding alpaca, harvesting potatoes, spinning and weaving—the Q'ero discuss the dreams of the night. In whispered voices, they huddle in their stone huts, wrapped in furs and woolen blankets, recounting tales of the dream world. The shaman or a wise elder may comment, though never in an opinionated or dominating manner, but gentle and encouraging in a sharing of the personal telling rather than an interpretive way.

To the Q'ero, dreams are listened to with a clear heart, not analyzed with a grasping mind.

Six months after our time together in Lima, while together with Sebastian and Nicolas in the Sacred Valley, I have a dream about meeting a Quechua holy man in Urubamba who reveals the secret of the Andes. A mosaic of wisdom rich in detail and at the same time veiled, my dream offers clues about ancient knowledge, yet in the morning the meaning is elusive. I am unable to recall the details. This bothers me and I resolve to make every effort to understand the teachings revealed to me.

~

A thin sickle of moon hangs in the dawn sky, silent and silver. Moonlight and night run into each other, a few stars linger in the darkness, the rising sun still well below the horizon. No wind stirs the trees; deep green leaves turn eastward waiting the sun. Nothing is completely pure in this life, but moments like this have a purity all their own.

"*Hatunmunaycha,*" Sebastian whispers in the dark. "Great beauty."

He is awake before me, sitting still, present with the night, facing east waiting the sun. We sit together without speaking, the darkness gradually fading towards cobalt gray, the first faint rays of sunlight coming over the surrounding hills.

Nicolas arrives, sleepy-eyed and smiling. At twenty-six, he is slightly taller than his father with the same oval face, well-defined nose, and intense dark brown eyes characteristic of Andean Quechua people, but with a softer look more like his mother. He has the presence of a shaman even before completing full initiation rites as if he were born to the role. He shows a keen sensibility for the Apus and Pachamama, and holds a fierce loyalty to his shamanic lineage, while embracing a modern future. As a natural leader, Nicolas relies on his Inkan origins that run deep in his blood and this often means hours of discussion that culminate in mutual understanding that reaches across culture and time.

"*Pichukuka*" Sebastian says. "Let's share coca leaves."

Chapter Two: The Teaching of Suryamana

In the Andes, everything begins and ends with coca, and important dreams are no exception. Nicolas readies a place on the grass for us to sit around an uncuño of natural brown, black, white, and grey colored alpaca wool representing the four *suyus* of the Inkan empire: the cardinal directions of north, south, east, and west.

He sits, adjusts his poncho, and piles coca leaves on the uncuño to prepare for ritual sharing. Sebastian wears his daily *punchu,* the hand woven beige-colored natural alpaca wool poncho typical of the Q'ero with its thin double line of deep red strips woven along the borders that remind me of the markings on the heads of Sandhill cranes. His ch'ulhu, the brightly colored wool cap worn in the Andes, lays aside, his crow black hair, cropped short with a dull knife, silken and askew.

We sit cross-legged in a triangle, knee to knee, bonding with plant and spirit, listening to each other, non-judgmental, to determine what we may accomplish together for the greater good in harmony with a design other then our own.

Coca leaf sharing is an act of Ayni that clarifies the mind and calms the heart. It requires the willingness to allow thoughts and events to evolve according to their own timing. We each form k'intus, choosing three perfectly shaped leaves symbolizing the threefold level of existence, as an offering of reciprocity to the Apus. Coca forms the bridge between human consciousness and the intelligence of the Apus. Green and dry as toast with a distinctive aromatic earthy fragrance, not sweet but unique; just as nothing else has the aroma of coffee or chocolate, so too coca has a scent of its own.

The only sound is the faint rustling of leaves as Sebastian lifts handfuls of coca and lets them slip through his fingers, repeatedly sifting through them looking for the most perfectly formed ones. He is the first to raise a k'intu to his lips. Mind one-centered, eyes closed, he recites the names of the Apus from every journey we have been on together, and raising the k'intu to the sky, blows three times into the leaves, uniting his breath with the mountain spirits, the sky, and the stars.

While he prays, I am silent; my mind moves into this stillness. Uramama, mother coca, is present. Reverence exists as we sort leaves, selecting only the perfect ones, preparing for the phukuyr'tti. The last moments of night turn the cobalt sky translucent before slipping into morning. Apu Chicon, the guardian spirit of Urubamba, gradually becomes visible, its snow and ice ageless, and I raise my k'intu to honor the mountain spirit.

"Apu Chicon, apu pumahuanca, apu pitusiray, apu sawasiray, come into this moment. Fill this silence with your presence. Find us willing and ready to serve for the good of the people. Come mountain spirits. Come Pachamama." Sebastian prays.

Nicolas bows his head, and holding his k'intu lightly between thumb and forefinger close to his heart, attunes to his father's invocation and our purpose. For this moment, he dedicates his entire being. A dream is about to be told, a tale spun, history made.

After Sebastian's invocation, we present k'intus to each other, each whispering prayers to the Apus, and perform the phukuyr'tti, ritual blowing of the breath—the life force, *kallpa*—into the coca. Then, placing the leaves in our mouths, chew ever so slowly, careful not to grind the dry leaves into sharp pieces that cut gums and irritate the throat, but masticating unhurriedly to extract the juice that contains the active principles, which the Q'ero consider the essence of coca they respectfully call uramama.

Whole dried coca leaves[6] contain small amounts of cocaine, but also a number of other alkaloids including nicotine. When carefully chewed, there is a mild stimulant effect that suppresses hunger, thirst, pain, fatigue, and cold. Communal chewing in the Andes dates back at least 8,000 years, and very likely is even more ancient. To the Q'ero, coca links the individual to the Apus and knits the community to Pachamama.

Though the clarifying effect of coca sharpens my mind, the dream is slipping away and memory comes in fragments. What I say is not what I experienced; my words lack substance, the recounting is limited by my inability to remember, and the details dissolve before I can speak them.

Chapter Two: The Teaching of Suryamana

By their expressions, I know Sebastian and Nicolas sense my dilemma and intuitively recognize that the import of the dream requires action, telling is not sufficient.

"That was an Apu," Nicolas offers, his words on point, his expression attentive, looking to his father for approval and clarification.

"An Apu in a dream is a good sign," Sebastian agrees, his eyes gleam, his pupils large round agates.

"It could mean that you are to meet such a man," Nicolas offers, and suggests that I might learn further lessons in other dreams in the future.

They are the dream masters, so I listen attentively, but worry that I will not remember clearly enough, and with each passing minute as the sun rises and the sky turns blue, my memory moves towards transparent.

Dreams can be many-layered, each containing a unique meaning that resists easy explanation. The Q'ero way is to let the dream live. Explore it as one would a new country, one step at a time, stopping here and there to take in the lay of the land. This is also the approach taken by James Hillman,[7] the American psychologist considered by some the successor to Carl Jung, and one radically different from Sigmund Freud, the father of psychoanalysis. Hillman's approach accepts dreams as having a reality of their own and he does not confine them to interpretation. In this way, he and Sebastian would see eye to eye, or rather, dream to dream.

"It can mean many things," Nicolas continues. "Sometimes, when a real place is recognized within the dream, it helps to go there. Since your dream took place in Urubamba, let's go to town and see if you can remember the dream better. We can follow where it leads us."

"*Haku*," Sebastian announces, getting up and grabbing his bundle he makes for the door. "Let's go."

∾

It is mid-morning as we walk uphill along Calle Simon Bolivar, a narrow cobble stoned street named for the Venezuelan idealist who liberated South America from the grip of inquisitional Spain. We are in no rush and stop from time to time along the way; the farther we go, the slower we walk. Framed at the end of a narrow side street along our path, a waning ghost of a crescent moon lingers translucent in the eastern sky. The snowy top of Apu Chicon peers triangular over the tiled rooflines in front of us, distant by hours on foot but its image immediate and powerful as we walk toward the Plaza de Armas, the small park that forms the social center of Urubamba.

"Apus are not just mountains," Sebastian states.

His words redirect my awareness from the moon and mountain to the present. A lesson is about to begin, and I become alert, listening. In Q'ero style, Sebastian imparts wisdom in layers like weaving; one fine thread of knowledge follows another. If distracted, the message can be missed, the knowledge imparted is then in danger of becoming disconnected from Pachamama's loom of wholeness.

For the Q'ero, true knowledge, *yachay,* comes from direct personal experience guided by intuition, quickened by the Apus. The Q'ero way is a *coming into knowing,* rather than a mere accumulation of facts, or the amassing of experiences. But unless infused with *munay,* the essence of love and beauty, and enlivened by insight, knowledge tends to become fragmented and useless, or worse, a misleading distortion of ego and imagination.

Speaking of mountains as if they are people and stones as neighbors, the conversation warms and we walk so close, we bump shoulders in order to hear each other, our words whispered to keep strangers, people and spirits, from listening in.

"Hai!" I answer. "An Apu is the indwelling spiritual presence of the snow-capped mountain peaks."

"True," Nicolas says taking care that his words come clear. "You already know a lot about the Apus, but there is more. The Apus *speaks* to the pakuq."

Pakuq is Quechua for an Andean shaman-priest, like his father who is a ceremonialist called a pampamisayoq, initiated in the service of Pachamama, guided by the *apukuna* and *awkikuna*.

"An Apu can change form. One minute it is a condor, or a hummingbird, and next the wind." Nicolas comments.

"I understand," I tell him. Listening deeply, I imagine the moon takes a deep interest in our discussion. "Apus are more than the manifestation of things. An Apu is a powerful being, an expression of consciousness as clear intense intelligence on Earth, and this intelligence can be communicated through dreams, by animals or insects, wind or thunder, or to humans through intuition."

"You have learned well, Santiago," Nicolas says, and Sebastian nods in agreement, "but there is more…our altomisayoqs teach that the spirit of an Apu is pure white light."

An altomisayoq is a master shaman, the highest level of pakuq. He, or she, receives initiation directly from Apu Ausangate, the greatest of all Apus, and has the power to summon the spirit of an Apu into material form. In Peru, there are few altomisayoqs left. Even among the Q'ero, the acknowledged last ancestors of the Inkas, only two remain.

We pause, standing side by side, looking up at the snow covered peak of Apu Chicon framed by a blue more like the sea than the sky. I realize that there is no end to learning the Q'ero way of knowledge. This is one of those moments when dream and reality, memory and immemorial time, ancient past and modern present, merge into the same stream of consciousness. Moments become months. Hours become minutes. Seconds turn into a limitless realm of myth and magic, and timeless beauty.

∼

When you go from the wintery landscape of Cusco at 10,800 and descend to 9,400 feet, it makes for perpetual spring in the Sacred Valley. Brown hilltops give way to terraced mountain sides, avocado and fig trees bear fruit all year, and wildflowers grace the river banks. Sunlight filters through clouds of butterflies. Stalks of corn grow tall along the river bottom. The Inkas favored its gentler climate, compared to the higher elevations, and I am comfortable here, yet powerful unseen currents still play in the fields of the mountain spirits, archetypal ore laying rich veins in the subconscious.

A spiritual sleeping volcano, Urubamba is dormant with implications. The town lies in a protected pocket at a right angle to the Urubamba River, which flows north through the Sacred Valley towards the base of Machu Picchu. Across the river, a high bluff rises upward to form a plateau where potatoes, barley, and fava beans are grown on rolling plains belonging to the communities of Chincero and Maras. The town sits on a sloping fertile valley in front of snow-capped Apu Chicon at 18,150 feet, flanked by Apus Pitusiray and Sawasiray to the south and Pumahuanca to the north.

In Inkan times, Urubamba was a thriving city built around *Q'espiwanka,* a palace laced with springs and fountains built for Wayna Capac, "Splendid Youth," the eleventh Sapa Inka (1464-1527) and the father of Atahualpa, who was ransomed and murdered by Francisco Pizarro. Wayna Capac died of small pox, a fatal viral disease that preceded the Spaniards. More trouble was brewing. While fighting to expand the Inkan Empire in current day Ecuador, Atahualpa's half brother, Huàscar, in alliance with the Spanish fought against his father and brother for the Empire.

History informs us that Wayna Capac was capable, handsome, and charming. As a fierce warrior and skilled strategist he expanded the empire to its full extension from Quito, Ecuador to northern Chile. He mingled with the people and was admired and loved by all. When not at war, he enjoyed bathing in the pure water that flowed through Q'espiwanka from springs on the mountain slopes, the baths lavished with fresh flowers. Remnants of the palace, and its extensive irrigation system with some canals still in use, remain as a reminder of long ago, while the inlaid stone streets of Inkan times abide in a town that is now crumbling in disrepair.

The central park of Peruvian towns is called the Plaza de Armas. Urubamba's plaza is graced with red and yellow *kantutas*[8] the sacred flower of the Andes and national flower of Peru, and surrounded with jacaranda trees laden with purple blossoms dropping petals that drift through the plaza. Freshly painted green benches spaced around the plaza make convenient oases for people-watching, and intimate conversation.

As we approach the plaza, I suddenly pause. Something unseen alerts my senses, and then I am standing under a waterfall, bathed in image after image of my dream. Sebastian, noticing my change in mood, suggests we sit on one of the green benches so I can continue talking about the dream in a more relaxed manner. We choose a quiet part of the plaza and sit side-by-side on an empty bench facing a small church, the *Templo San Pedro Urubamba*.

I am absorbed in munay, the lightness of being that natural beauty creates in moments of spiritual attunement. In perfect harmony, I begin to recount to the best of my ability what I remember.

Sebastian looks at me with an expressionless gaze. But his eyes, dark and reflective as polished obsidian, are fierce and penetrating as if examining my soul.

"The dream began near here. There were fewer and fewer people in the park until there was no one at all. No taxis or trucks plied the narrow streets; not even a dog barked; there was no wind, and the sky was empty of birds. The small church, up the street in front of us, was undergoing repairs. Inkan stones used for the foundation were laid bare as layers of old stucco were removed, yet there were no workmen in sight. The Plaza de Armas, typically full of curious children, was empty. The entire town, momentarily deserted, lay quiet and still..."

Details come back, not all at once, but piece by piece, however this time in an order that by linking images together I remember more detail than in the morning, and—all at once—a torrent of memories. While sitting on the green wooden bench in Urubamba, the moon, faintly visible in the morning sky fades into the clouds and the sun moves higher passing closer to overhead, as I recount the whole dream in detail.

A man walks down the center of the street ahead of us toward the church, and other than Nicolas and

I, and the man, there is no one in the plaza or on the street: no dogs bark, no taxis ply the avenues, no children play, no older women peer out windows. We are intent on finding someone, so Nicolas suggests we ask the man for information. We hurry to catch up to him, but no matter how fast we walk, and how slow he strolls, we get no closer. We pick up our pace cutting through the park to intercept him, but cannot close the distance. The man stops in the middle of the street in front of the church, as if allowing us to catch up with him. As we approach, he turns his head side ways toward us, not all the way, just enough not to see his face.

"*Buenas dias,*" he says in formal Castellan. "In what way may I be of help? Perhaps you are looking for someone?"

"*Si tio,*" I answer politely, "Thank you for your help. We heard about a man who lives near here who is knowledgeable in the old ways. Maybe you have heard of him?"

I feel my way through the dream like a writer who goes over his work line by line, and as we sit in the park and I look at the church in front of us, I wonder if there is a connection between waking reality, as Nicolas suggested earlier, and my dream. These are moments when non-ordinary reality blends with normal waking reality, and dreams become real. Knowing that Nicolas and Sebastian are looking for that link as well, I glance over at them for a clue, but Nicolas is straight-faced, though not as stoic as his father, with just the hint of a smile at the corners of his lips. Sebastian's face is unreadable. There will be no help from these two, so I begin again.

"Ah, yes, I know of this man," he replies, pointing to the right of the church, giving us vague directions, but in great detail: "He lives not too far, but not to close from here, and to that side of the church, and a little beyond." The man goes on like this for some time.

"Have a good day," he says when finished giving directions and walks off.

All of a sudden, people are in the street and children play on the benches in the park. An older woman stands in a doorway talking with another woman. A few dogs chase after each other along the sidewalk, and taxi drivers lean on their newly polished cars eyeing us as prospective passengers. This happens so abruptly that I take no notice of the man, and when I look for him, he is gone without a trace.

Nicolas and I start off past the church as the man indicated and although the directions he gave us are complicated, we have no difficulty remembering them. We go along the right side of the church; then walk a few blocks and turn down a side street too narrow for even a small car to pass. As we walk it becomes narrower, almost claustrophobic, and the buildings appear older, not Inkan but colonial Spanish, as if, with each block, we are walking back in time. We come to the edge of town, cross over an ancient stonework irrigation system running with cold water from the mountains flowing fast in its stone channel and the crooked plank that serves as a foot bridge shaking like a leaf as we cross. Then, we continue along a narrow footpath winding between stone and adobe houses with grass thatching for roofs until we come to the one the man described to us.

The one room hut made of dark grey stones, abode blocks, and immense carved stones that form the foundation with one wall composed of a single stone slab, is set off the path in a basin of tall grass and wild flowers surrounded by giant rocks up ended pointing skyward. The door, crooked on the frame, is ajar. We walk up to it and as I knock, Nicolas calls a greeting in Quechua.

A voice from within answers and invites us to enter. We peer in to the hut and see a man with his back to us tending a blackened pot over a crude fireplace set to one side against the far wall. Like most Andean traditional dwellings, smoke vents through a hole in the roof making the place smell of centuries of wood and earth and fire.

He turns to greet us, and we see that it is the same man from the street, but now dressed differently. When we met him in front of the church, he wore dark trousers and jacket, as if he had just came from attending Mass. Now he wears a plain white long-sleeve cotton shirt and over it a vest the orange and yellows of sunset. For pants he wears traditional short leggings hand woven from alpaca wool of such a dark brown that they are almost black. For footwear he has on rough sandals, the preferred wear for Andean natives, the same style that Sebastian always wears but his are made the old way with alpaca skin and sinew. On his head he wears the traditional knitted cap, but the color of stone and sod instead of the bright red and yellow ones typically worn in the Andes with colors and patterns distinctive for each region making his place of origin hard to determine. His poncho, draped over a chair, is an intense dark blue with fine lines of turquoise and red near the borders. Intricate diamond designs of sage green and earth tones compose the center. The craftsmanship is impressive. I have never seen such colors or designs before in Peru, except in museums, the ancient Inkan textiles finely crafted compared to the coarser work of today.

"You were called by your dream," he speaks to me in Quechua, which I understand perfectly.

"Are you surprised?" he questions as if in answer to my thoughts. "You have been on this path for a long time and should be familiar with such events."

True, I have had many encounters with non-ordinary reality before in Peru, which I term the Peruvian enigma, so my surprise is momentary, but such encounters are always new and different each time, and for a moment I lose my sense of equilibrium.

I pause to catch my breath. Sebastian was right: it is easier to remember a dream when assisted by the affinity of place. While sitting in the park with my companions at my side, I am more at ease. Closing my eyes, I continue describing the dream, images spilling like water through my mind.

"I knew you might come but needed to be sure that you found me. Time is urgent. That's why I met you in the street," the man continues still tending the fire with his back to us.

Sunlight, more intense as morning approaches noon, enters diagonally through two small windows on the west side of the room, and filtered by the smoke from the fire, gives the room a bluish aura. As my eyes adjust to the curious color, I see the room is empty except for a very small wooden table and three chairs. The north wall, built around an ancient structure of huge rectangular grey stones cut with the usual precision so apparent in all Inkan stonework, contains a recessed altar space is adorned with red kantutas, a round dark stone the size of a small egg, and coca leaves. The uneven dirt floor tips the table to one side, and next to one of the three chairs is the man's *q'epe,* the Andean carrying bundle, the same natural color as his cap.

The man adds coca leaves and fresh herbs to the boiling water he is tending, and Nicolas and I, still standing by the door, watch him closely as he drops one leaf at a time into the water. Without breaking his attention to the *mate de coca,* Andean coca leaf tea, he invites us to sit.

Nicolas and I sit down, and I run the soles of my shoes over the hard-packed earthen floor. I feel the firmness of the earth and it seems to settle me. The dream is so real that it has taken on a texture of its own that makes the line between realities so thin there is no distinction at all.

When the mate is finished, he steps away from the fire, pours three earthenware cups full of steaming tea that smell of turned soil and roots and plants, and serves us at the table. We wait to drink until he is ready; the dark green leaves floating in our cups turn brown from the hot water.

Nicolas looks at me with his coffee-colored eyes, and nods ever so slightly. An offering is in order. I take from my daypack a translucent green plastic bag filled with coca leaves and hand them to him, which he gives to the man using both hands offered in the traditional Andean gesture of goodwill.

Our gift of coca leaves to one side of the table, we raise our cups, but before drinking pour a small amount of the mate onto the dirt floor as a symbolic act of respect, an expression of Ayni to Pachamama, then drink in silence.

When we finish, the man clears the table and unfolds an uncuño, sky blue with an earth-colored border and a forest green, *chakana,* Andean cross, in the center. Two thin reddish brown lines divide it into four equal quadrants.

He reaches into the bag of coca leaves we gave him and selects nine leaves and forms them into three k'intus; touching them to his lips, he blows gently on them, and walks to the stone wall where he places them in the altar space pausing a moment to whisper a prayer.

Returning to the table, he takes a handful of his own coca leaves, larger and greener and more perfectly shaped than ours, and places them on the uncuño with a hand gentle from long experience of touching the textures of the earth. He selects another three k'intus from among his leaves and hands one to Nicolas, then passes another to me, keeping one for himself.

I watch Nicolas for clues to proper etiquette. He holds his k'intu, greener side facing his heart, and following his lead hold mine between the first two fingers of both hands, greener side inward, preparing my heart and mind for the blessing, breath by breath, trying to stay calm, but all the while electrified with expectation.

Taking his k'intu, the man lifts them to his lips and performs the phukuyr'tti, the sacred blowing of one's breath of life into the coca leaves, the sacred plant of the Andes, the bridge between the Apus and the human mind, and in a voice resonant of steep canyons bordered by high mountain walls, he invokes the apukuna naming each as one would old friends.

"Earth spirits from Bolivia, Lake Titicaca, of Cuzco, and Q'ero, and beyond; from the heart of Urubamba, I invite you to awaken and listen:

Apu pitusiray, apu sawasiray, apu colequecruz, apu condorwachana, apu pumahuanca, amaruhaunca, apu qolqeconoqa, apu chicon, apu salkantay, apu wakawillqa, apu halancoma, apu huanacauri, apu putucusi, apu waynapichu, apu machu picchu, apu pachatusan, apu ausangate, hanpuy hanpuy."

Holding our leaves to our lips, Nicolas and I with eyes closed perform the phukuyr'tti, aligning our will, energy, and hearts with the Apus.

When we open our eyes, the man is standing in front of us, eyes closed and heart wide open, the center of his chest aglow with a translucent emerald green light. Six coca leaves are fixed between his fingers and in a whispered voice he prays in an ancient tongue that even Nicolas does not understand. He finishes his invocation and cups his hands around the leaves, and holding them to his chest in front of his heart, the green light infuses the coca leaves.

Taking a single leaf, he gently crushes it to powder. Bending down, he sprinkles the green powder on the earthen floor, uttering a prayer in the ancient language. The second leaf he also crushes to powder and blows it into the air around our heads; I hear wings, an intensely soft sound as when a bird flies close to your head. The third leaf he places in his mouth and chews slowly. The remaining three leaves he places on the uncuño in the center of the table.

Following his example, we pray, blow three times onto our k'intus, and then place our leaves in our mouths and chew.

As he sits down, I see his eyes for the first time: deep as rivers and dark as forests. I go breathless under his gaze, and as in a trance, a dream within the dream, I see mountain after snow-capped mountain, and I am soaring over them like a condor.

"I am Suryamana," I hear him say as if from a great distance. Instantly, I am back in the room at the table. "I have knowledge beyond human belief. I come from a secret and inaccessible place deep in these mountains. The mysteries that conceal this knowledge have been guarded for five hundred years. But times have changed. There is almost no one left to carry the sacred stones that hold the key to these mysteries. We are concerned for the fate of the world."

Sitting beside Nicolas and Sebastian on the green bench in the plaza in Urubamba, the dream takes on a reality of its own, and I become lost in the telling. Nicolas turns to me; his eyes are brilliant and expectant. Sebastian is still and silent, listening deeply, feeling his way through the dream with me.

Continuing, I recount how everything in the dream turns spontaneously inward as in deep meditation. The light filtered by the smoke from the now dying fire facilitates mind expansion; I am transported in time and space and brought to a state of knowing by Suryamana's words. The dream becomes tangible. It is much more than recalling memories—images flood my mind, my words race to keep up with them.

There are moments in the presence of spiritual masters when everything heard makes perfect sense, rings true, and all questions are answered so clearly and simply you wonder why you didn't think of it before. Things flow to their rightful places like water gathers into pools after a rain. However, by the next morning you can't remember what you heard and no matter how hard you try the understanding so perfectly in place the day before seems remote and as unfathomable as ever. With each passing day, the memory fades like a ship sailing towards the horizon, becoming smaller and smaller until there is only the tiniest speck...and you stand on the shore watching it disappear...forever.

I fear that these are such moments, but go on the best that I can, recounting as much of the dream as possible to Nicolas and Sebastian.

"We are at a turning point," Suryamana speaks. "Some call it a crisis point, but it is more than that. These are transformational times. There is much to learn, but little time to teach it. I speak about what is most important, not leaving anything out, and keep it as simple as possible so you can understand. The rest you will learn when you return to the high mountains where you will experience directly from Pachamama and the great Apu."

As he talks, thunder rolls over the mountains from the direction of Apu Pitusiray rumbling into the village and to the door of the hut, and though desperate to learn, the thunder is so loud I cannot hear him.

The last words I remember are: "The fundamental point is Ayni."

Suryamana stands, walks to the altar space with the same deliberation as when handling the coca leaves but instead of reaching for the oval stone, he holds his palms facing each other a few inches apart and the stone rises up and hovers between his hands. Then he closes his palms around the stone, touches it to his chest in front of his heart, walks to the table and placing the stone and the three coca leaves on his uncuño, carefully folds it, and puts it into his carrying bundle, slips on his blue poncho, and slinging his bundle over his shoulder, heads out the door.

"We will see each other again," he calls without

turning around as he walks towards the mountains in the last light of afternoon, thunder rolling out of the sky.

"When?" I call after him.

"Soon," I hear him say, and he keeps going without looking back.

∼

Sebastian and Nicolas listen for more than an hour, no questions from these two. Nicolas quietly translates from Spanish to Quechua the entire time, his softly spoken words parallel my telling without breaking the story. Sebastian remains attentive, his eyes never once wandering from mine. Neither of them interrupts nor comments during my telling, and when I finish, Sebastian and Nicolas discuss things for some time before speaking to me.

"That was not a person," Nicolas says gently. "There is no question. We are certain, it was an Apu."

"Your dream is clear, Santiago, but there are unanswered questions and parts you do no remember," Sebastian says. "Let's try to find this place. Haku."

It is afternoon now and the day is warmer and clouds are moving along the valley and entering the spaces between the mountain walls. As we set off towards the church, Nicolas walks ahead of Sebastian and I, and speaking to the caretaker finds that there is a ruin nearby, once a sacred Inkan shrine according to the caretaker that Nicolas says may be worth exploring.

As we pass by, the caretaker, an older man sweeping the sidewalk to the right side of the church, stops his work to discretely talk with Sebastian in Quechua. Nicolas and I wait to the side. The caretaker looks at me while talking with Sebastian, and then he points up the street towards the mountains. I thank him, though I had not heard a word he said to Sebastian, and we head along Calle Grau, a narrow concrete street framed with blue, white, and yellow stucco buildings in various stages of decay, the paint faded and peeling from wear and exposure.

Winding through side streets, one narrower than the other, we continue towards the mountains, until the tightly packed dwellings of the town turn to more open spaces interspersed with individual houses scattered along a dirt road full of pot holes that have not been filled in years. A narrow irrigation canal runs deep alongside the road and Sebastian instinctively follows as it bends off the road to our right. Nicolas and I step quickly along behind him, walking single file along a narrow path to the side of the canal. There are gardens and fields, and as we move higher, the tile rooftops of the town are visible below us. We soon come to a rough wooden plank crossing the canal. Intuitively, I indicate that we should cross here, and in about twenty-five yards come to a stone house set among what appears to be Inkan ruins.

The ruins are like my dream but smaller, overgrown with bushes and opportunistic grass bunching up everywhere. What is left of a structure built around Inkan stones is largely collapsed and the door, long removed from its hinges, lays askew on the ground. The yard is littered with gravel and rubble, and a few discarded plastic bottles lay discolored and crumpled, but some one has brought wild flowers and laid them in the shrines.

"Look here," Sebastian says, pointing to a rock carved like the head of a snake."

This is a place of water, *uño,* sacred to the Inkas and all Andeans. I make out channels and passages leading through stone and earth that once was a *huaca,* a place where the awkikuna, nature spirits, dwell. The snake, *amaru,* represents water and the underworld in Andean mythology, *ukhupacha,* and is regarded as a power of transformation, symbolizing wisdom gained from overcoming one's own dark side, the psychological fears and unsettling behavior that prevents us from experiencing the light and beauty of munay. In Inkan times, a carved image of a snake over a door or near the entrance of temples revealed a place dedicated to wisdom keepers, *yachaywasikuna.* This may have been such as place more than five hundred years ago.

Sebastian takes off his poncho, enters into the remains of the house, and spreading it on the ground, beckons us to sit with him.

He positions an uncuño in front of us and taking coca from his bundle piles a large amount of dried green leaves in the center. We have been talking and walking all morning, now it is time to center ourselves, clarify our minds, and tune into the sacred space around us reaching deep in order to learn the lesson of the dream.

He sorts the leaves by lifting them up in small bunches and lets them drift downward onto the uncuño, falling as they will. In the apparent randomness of the falling leaves, he reads signs made by patterns and shapes of individual leaves. He picks up a few unusually shaped ones and comments upon their meaning.

"This one tells of a journey. This one is strangely shaped but symmetrical and means the journey will be important and all will go well."

Now he chooses a specific number of leaves all about the same size, then blows into them and prays, and puts them down in a rapid series of wrist flicks, commenting during the process: "It is good. This place is good."

The last few leaves form a spiral turning into a pattern all their own. *"Anchahatun,* very big energy," he says pushing back from the coca.

Nicolas and I choose our k'intus. I find three perfectly shaped and matching leaves of the same size, and lay them to the side, and choose additional ones.

Sebastian takes three k'intus, nine leaves in three pairs, as in my dream, and performs the phukuyr'tti. Then he gets up and places them in what appears to be the main shrine, honoring the possibility that this may indeed have been the place in my dream.

Nicolas goes outside and collects wild flowers and offers them along with his coca leaves, placing them along side his father's coca leaves.

I take up my misa, the sacred bundle of Q'ero shamanism, and twelve k'intus and knelling, face Apus Chicon, Pitusiray, and Sawasiray and pray as I remember in the dream calling the mountain spirits to manifest their presence now and in our lives.

Apu pitusiray, apu sawasiray, apu colequecruz, apu condorwachana, apu pumahuanca, apu amaruhaunca, apu qolqeconoqa, apu chicon, apu salkantay, apu wakawillqa, apu halancoma, apu huanacauri, apu putucusi, apu waynapichu, apu machu picchu, apu pachatusan, apu ausangate, hanpuy hanpuy.

A light rain spatters the dirt outside and the sky turns deep purple as the sun nears the high plateau to the west, layers of dark clouds hide the mountains behind, and fill the valley with a blanket of gray. It is certain to rain hard in the night, maybe even snow on the peaks.

As I finish, we exhale as one and in the silence between breaths there is no sound. Nicolas is motionless. I follow his gaze out the stone window.

Dragonflies have come to the openings and hover blue-headed with translucent golden wings dazzling in the late afternoon as the sun breaks through the clouds for a few moments of light before dropping below the mountains for the night.

I stand slowly so as not to disturb them and stooping low pass through the stone doorway. As I step away from the hut, hundreds of dragonflies circle within two feet of my head. There is a humming sound emitted from their wings, like the engine of the universe. I close my eyes, being careful not to blink so as not to frighten them, fold my hands in prayer to the center of my chest and bow to the Apus, humbled by the beauty of the experience and the indefinable nature of my dream, thankful for this touch of spirit.

Sebastian and Nicolas watch without blinking, faces framed by the open window. Every thing in the world stands still. The dragonflies encircle closer almost touching my face. Then they disperse at an astonishing speed and fly in all directions. In a moment they are gone.

"Hatunmunaycha!" Sebastian exclaims breaking the silence. "Great beauty! It is time. We have waited patiently. You have given to others for long enough. It is your time now. The signs are powerful and beautiful. Prepare yourself for your next initiation."

"Santiago, you are entrusted with a quest for knowledge. The Q'ero will help you," Nicolas says. "I and my father will make the necessary preparations for the journey."

As evening works its way towards night, we head down hill towards the church, circling around to the front, cross the street, and walk through the plaza until we find an empty bench to sit and ponder the day's events. Clouds descend down the mountain and almost touch the ground. It is cold now, but there is no wind, and for just a few minutes a light, soft snow falls, ephemeral flakes in a diagonal dance drift across the plaza melting as soon as they touch the ground.

We sit together on the green bench. In the long silence, the clouds clear and the first stars appear. The Southern Cross, best seen in early May, becomes visible. The moon, so present earlier in the day, will not rise for another few hours. Its absence makes the early night sky clear and the stars, white and crystalline.

∼

Two weeks later, back in Cusco, an event occurs that will shape the course of my life. Just as the dream pointed out the way of our journey, so this new experience gave the direction. Like the dream, it comes unexpected, and it tips my sense of the real toward a separate reality. Though my heart is at peace, my mind is restless and it questions what happened in Urubamba. I have doubts about the dream and the validity of its meaning. I am not content to let it be, to live out its own process, and am confused about what I have to do, and where I have to go.

When in Cusco, I rent a small two-room apartment several blocks above the *Plaza de San Francisco* near Calle Nueve Alta and not far from the central market. The front of the building is a girls' preparatory school built around a courtyard constructed by the Spanish in the early 1600's and who paved it with Inkan stones. A second story with a wood balcony surrounds the courtyard. Over the centuries, additional buildings have been tacked on to the original, once a grand structure but now laced with a labyrinth of causeways and catwalks where dozens of people live. To reach my apartment, I must pass through the main entrance into the school, walk under the balcony to the left of the courtyard; pass through a series of small doors, go along narrow open air corridors into a tiny courtyard, and then climb a rickety set of steps, more like a ladder than stairs, and along a creaking wooden catwalk. But my place is private and simple, and when school is out, it is quiet and a good place to meditate and write.

It is Sunday, so school is closed, and it has been raining all morning, the air crisp and wet, the streets slick with a fine layer of wet dust mixed with rain making a slippery surface of clay. I have been to the market for breakfast of Peruvian coffee and mountain bread and now I am making my way back to my apartment. I enter through a small door within the larger double doors, locked for the weekend but wide open during the week when school is in session; then walk down the central corridor, dark and damp from the rain. Water drips from the tile roof making a chorus of splashing sounds as it falls from above onto the stone walk.

The rain is slowing and the sun breaks through thinning clouds. As I enter the courtyard, a hole in the sky appears and a flash of brilliant Andean sunlight reflects off the roof tiles, the stone pavers glisten. I blink. Shading my eyes with my hand, I see a man through finger slits standing in the center of the courtyard.

Dressed in a common black and brown colored suit typical of Cusco, there appears nothing unusual about him other than the fact that he is alone and standing motionless in the rain in the center of the courtyard. I take another few steps towards my apartment, thinking I will ignore him, when I notice that he wears a traditional Quechua cap but in the ancient style of natural brown alpaca. I stop and turn to look at him. It is Suryamana, the man from my dream.

We face one another, I under the balcony, he in the rain. But I see that he is not wet even though it had been raining hard before and a light rain is still falling around him.

Motionless, hardly breathing, I watch while the image of the man

Chapter Two: The Teaching of Suryamana

becomes transparent until there is only scintillating light formed as if Suryamana is refracted in countless drops of rain; then he is gone. The rain stops and an intense Andean sun breaks through the remaining clouds, the wet tiles and stones shining. The last moments of my experience pulsate. It is simultaneously real and magical, profound and intense, and I am in the shimmer of rain and light playing upon my memory. My body quivers like the skin of a drum seconds after the final beat.

In the inner calm of closed eyes, I interlace my breath with heart beat, pausing to let my body relax on the exhalation, lingering on the out breath but without holding it, and then inhale the cold thin Andean air. I relax on the next exhalation, and then wait until the inhalation comes. I feel vibrantly alive.

I hear voices and footsteps on the stone pavers. Sebastian and Nicolas approach talking simultaneously in Quechua: the father calm and matter of fact; the son open-eyed and animated but with enough self-discipline to keep his voice down so as to not disturb the moment, which they sense but have not seen.

As I turn to greet them, Sebastian comes to me and looks up and into my eyes. He pauses, then turns and walks to the center of the courtyard looking down as if searching for footprints. Nicolas and I remain silent and unmoving. There are none, but he has to make sure.

A smell of kantutas lingers in the air, sweet and mixed with fresh rain.

"An Apu was here," Sebastian pronounces.

Nicolas is alert, looking at the rooflines, trying to catch a glimpse of something, a synchronicity of nature, the burst of a hummingbird.

Sebastian looks at me, his black hair glistening with rain, his dark brown eyes penetrating, unblinking. There is a brush of light rain and it polishes his face like water on stone. He looks up towards the sky.

The rain thins more and almost stops. I step beside Sebastian and facing in the same direction, he closes his eyes and bows, and I place my hands together in prayer palms warm, fingertips touching in front of my chest, heart and head and hands connecting, and bow to the Apus.

There is a sprinkling of mist out of a sun drenched blue sky. A rainbow appears arching up from the wet stone pavers where Suryamana stood before his image dissolved. We straighten together, eyes wide open, hearts expanding, the rainbow a few feet in front of us.

Nicolas goes out to the street to see where the rainbow ends as it arches up and over Cusco, towards the valley to the south. Sebastian and I stand looking up into the sky as the rainbow loses its color, fades transparent, and disappears.

He returns and speaks with his father, quietly off to the side. I catch only a few words, threads of meaning. Even Nicolas has trouble understanding his father sometimes. He questions Sebastian, again and again, until he gets it right. Then he picks up in Spanish for my benefit, slipping back in Quechua when the translation gets difficult.

"It's not easy to convey what my father is talking about," he explains, admitting that it is the first time he hears such things. The concepts are new to him and some of the words are in the ancient dialect, sacred runasimi. He pauses while they discuss more in Quechua. His face shows doubt and consternation. Is it because I am not one of them by ancestry, or is it because the subject is beyond his grasp?

For a moment, I wonder if he will continue.

"My father talks about an ancient and powerful ritual. It makes me so afraid that I am reluctant to translate. Many of the words he speaks are in the old way and I have to ask him many times to explain so that I have the meaning right."

Approaching me, Sebastian says in simple Quechua, "It is time. Apu Ausangate calls."

"We will prepare for your presentation to the Apu. It involves a powerful and dangerous ritual," Nicolas adds. "I have never participated in this type of ancient ceremony. It makes me afraid. You and my father have traveled together for many years. You and he are one soul in two bodies. I will help to organize and support your journey, but you and my father must go together again. Then

Chapter Two: The Teaching of Suryamana

you will go higher to face the Apu alone. Bring nothing but your misa and coca leaves."

Sebastian's nature is to cut through doubt and fear, and he brushes away concern: "There is nothing to fear."

I fall silent. Aware of the enormity of what we are to undertake, but willing to tremble on the mountain, a place invisible to the rest of the world, to make myself available to a moment of transport, where words, and even the perpetual inhabitants of the mind are without meaning, and only now matters. It is no longer about becoming. It is all about being.

Having long ago let go of the possibility of epiphany, I hope only to go and return, to present a good showing, to come back a better man, some of the darkness within me chiseled away; a little more self aware, with some thing new to give, and just perhaps something to say. But, right now, words are falling away like melting snow.

"Santiago," Sebastian says, "You don't choose the mountain. The Apu chooses you."

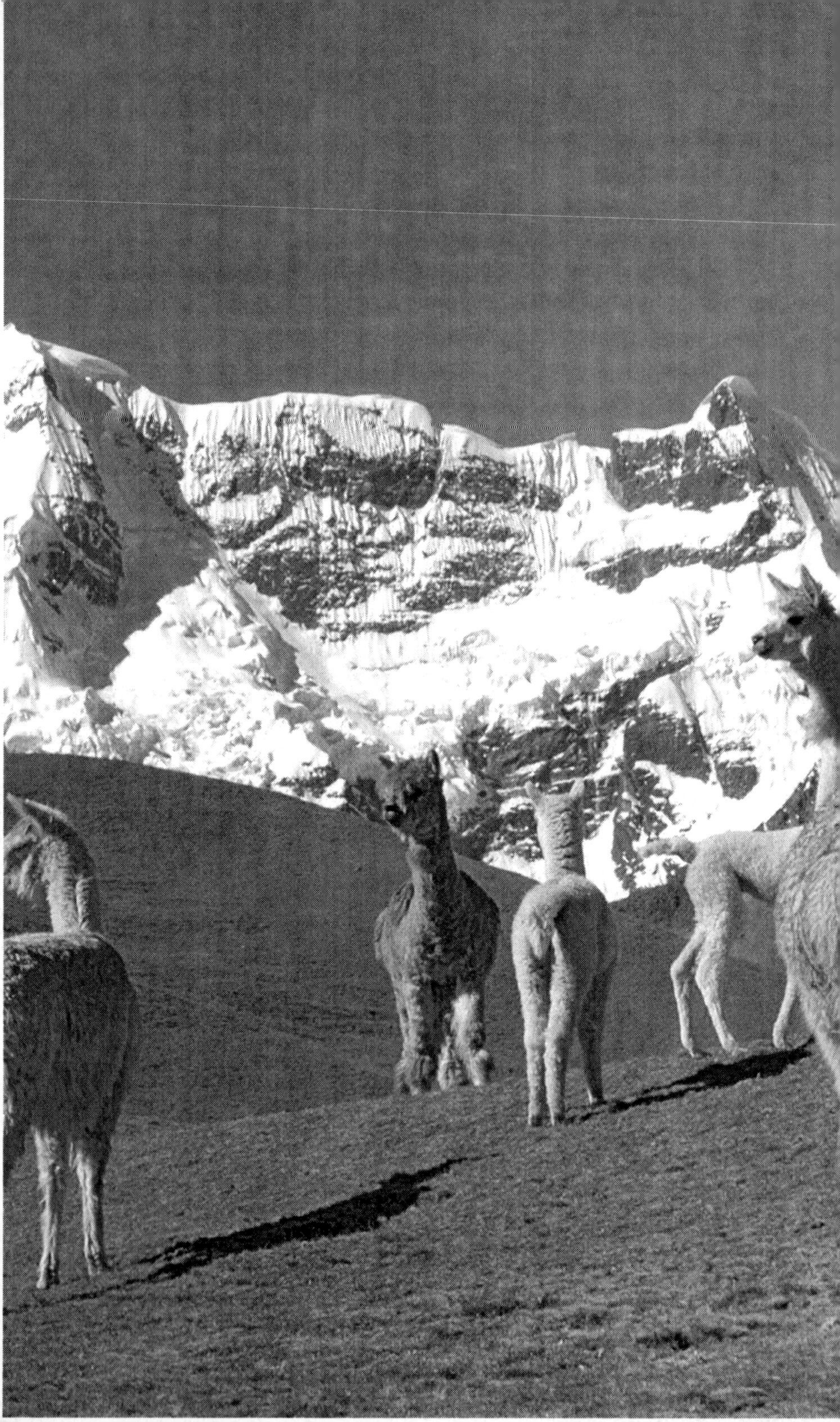

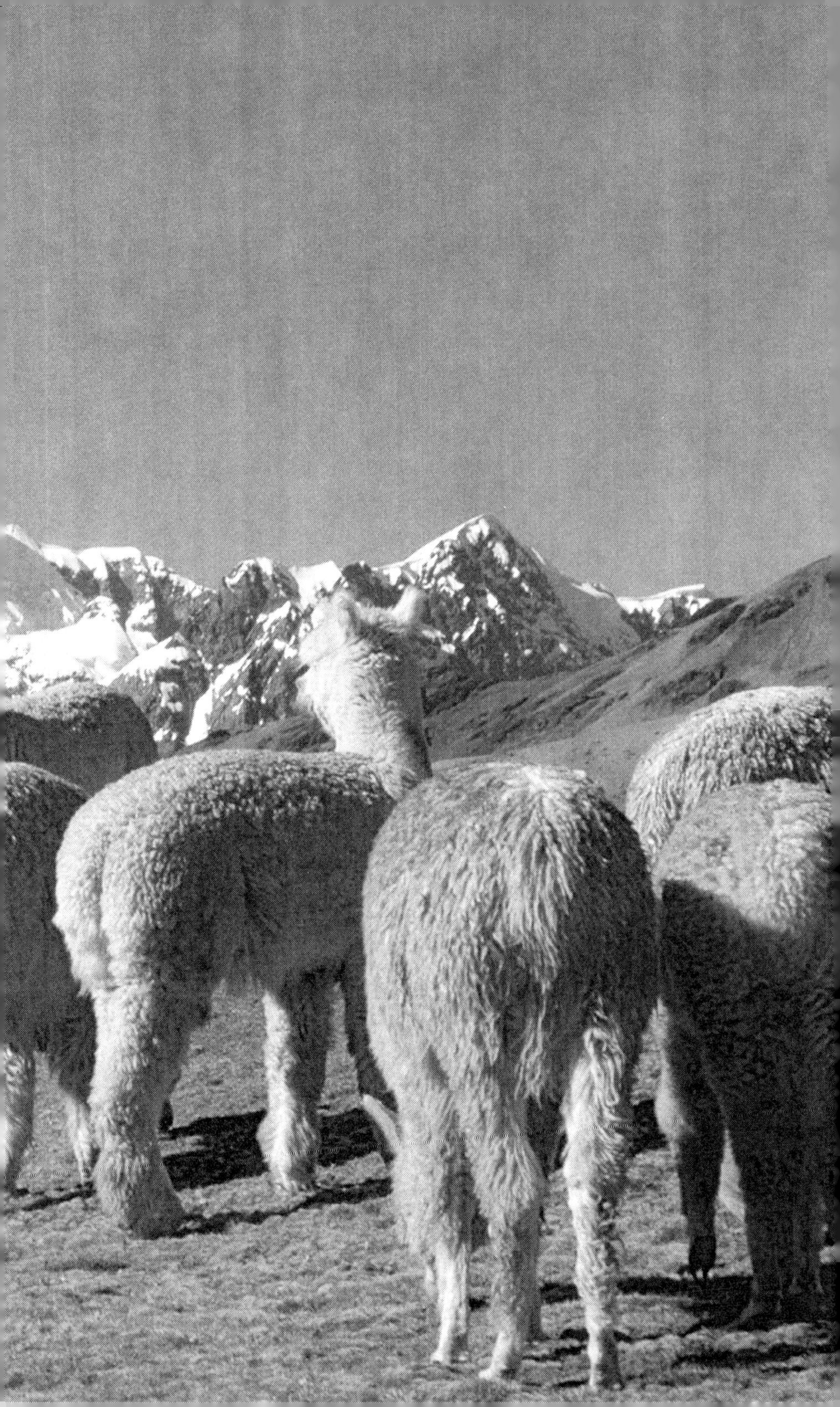

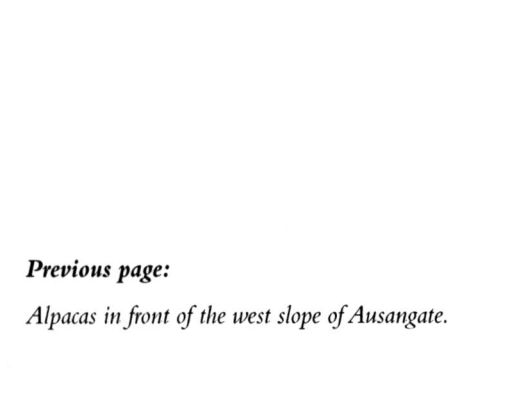

Previous page:
Alpacas in front of the west slope of Ausangate.

~ Chapter Three ~

THE THIN EDGE OF SILENCE

May 2008

A city of churches, Inkan stones, sky blue doors, old secrets and new truths, Cusco is more than its history. Though its origins may be Inkan, its magic is pre-Inkan, when it was called *Aqhamama*. Sebastian informs me that before the Inkas powerful shamans, masters of gravity, raised and moved the great stones in Sachsayhuaman by their energy alone. He claims this knowledge was inherited from even more ancient civilizations. Too much credit, he offers, is given to the Inkas. Nicolas adds that the shape of Cusco, designed before the Inkas, is that of a puma. The heart is located in the Qorikancha, where the Inkas kept the golden disc. The tail is in the shape of a serpent winding to the south, and the head in the form of a condor is Sachsayhuaman. The great stones he states were already in place when the Inkas arrived. Caverns and tunnels, and underground rivers and lakes connected them as a central nervous system of Cusco, and in one of these lakes still lies a sacred stone that once orchestrated it all.

The Western version of Inkan history is largely based on chronicles left by Spanish conquistadores. Such eyewitness accounts are fascinating, but colored by a European lens and limited because of inadequate knowledge of Quechua and a Catholic bias. None of the chronicles talk about the mystical traditions of the Andes. However, it is from these writings that we know Inkan civilization began with Manco Cápac and his consort, Mama Ocllo, who are believed to have claimed the Cusco valley as the "navel of the world." The fertile valley became the capital of the Inkan Empire, Tahuantinsuyu, the four corners of the world with Cusco at its umbilical center. Francisco Pizarro and his band of conquistadors arrived in Cusco for the first time in 1534, preceded by deadly epidemics and followed by decades of warfare leading to the collapse of the Inkan Empire.

Modern Cusco is a blend of underlying Inkan architecture, modified and built over in Spanish colonial style so that little of the original remains. Ramshackle adobe structures mushroom up the valley sides, expand directionless, and spill over into adjacent valleys. However, the city center remains largely unchanged and is as enchanting now as my first visit more than a decade earlier.

Sebastian, Nicolas, and I walk past the Plaza of San Francisco, down Marquez, and turn left at Calle Heladoeros. The church of Santa Teresa is framed at the end of the street by white stucco colonial buildings with blue balconies. A quiet park, the Plaza de Regocijo, canopied by trees planted around a circular fountain, is to our right. As we stroll through the plaza, even in Cusco people eye us.

I prefer listening to the Q'ero version of Andean history, and Sebastian talks on about pre-Inkan times. He has little sympathy for the Inkas. As we walk along, Nicolas and I listen to tales of power of pre-Inkan times.

We arrive at a café on a corner street. I feel at home here with Sebastian and Nicolas; they have become my family. I order mate de coca for us and it is a pleasure to sip the hot tea together. We reminisce about our first years together, and they fill me in on what has happened since my last visit.

The Dalai Lama was here with Tibetan lamas. They met with Q'ero elders, and Nicolas served as interpreter. I ask his impression of Tenzin Gyatso, The Fourteenth Dalai Lama, and he says: "The monk was not afraid to make a mistake." Profound, like seeing the universe in a raindrop, his Holiness' power of forgiveness extending to every one, including himself. I wish I could have more compassion for my own imperfections, to continue evenly in the face of repeated missteps and to move steadily forward when faced with tragedy or misfortune. There are many spiritual paths, I remind myself, but once your personal path is revealed, whether it is Tibetan Buddhism or Q'ero shamanism, you must travel it to the end, as perfectly and imperfectly as possible.

Over the next few weeks, we work on the construction plans for a cultural center, Ayniwasi – Reciprocity House – and when our responsibilities are done, make preparations to travel to one of the Earth's last sacred mountains, Apu Ausangate.

~

At 20,900 feet, Ausangate *(Ausan,* pronounced as-wan, means great transformation, and *gate,* pronounced gat-tay, means the primary or principle one) is the highest and largest massif in the southern Peruvian Andes.[9] It was the sacred mountain of the Inkas for all Tahuantinsuyu, and the people who lived here before them including the Q'ero who trace their history back more than 1,500 years. Unlike holy mountains in India and China, overlapped by centuries of gods, Ausangate is quickened by divinity itself. A tuning fork for a larger scale of events and history, Ausangate has served through countless millennia as a calling point where men who would be gods stood and listened.

To this day, for all Andean indigenous people, especially those in the Cusco region, Ausangate remains the most revered and feared of the Apus, the spiritual intelligence of the mountains that guides the destiny of people, events, and things. To the Q'ero, Apus are extraordinarily powerful and each has a specific power. The most powerful of all, Ausangate, is said to actually teach the shamanic way of knowledge to the dedicated pakuq.

Interestingly, the apukuna have relationships, and in this way they are like humans and animals. They have wives and children, brothers and sisters, and they interact with other mountains. According to Q'ero legend, Ausangate was one of three sons of a powerful ancient Apu named Atao Kuri. His brothers are Apus Ocongate and Kallangate. After a series of intense struggles, Ausangate emerged as the greatest of the three brothers, and became the highest of all mountains in the region. The wife of Ausangate is Maria Waymanlipa; their three children are Kamorana, Ahuanaco, and Allunhapa near Puno, in the vicinity of Lake Titicaca.

Ausangate is located fifty miles southeast of Cusco, but which feels much further because of the twisting dirt road that takes a half-day of dizzying driving to get even near. On a clear day, the mountain dominants the valley and appears close in the thin Andean atmosphere. However, it is almost always shrouded in dark mist or covered in thick clouds. Even close up, the clouds can be so dense you might not see it.

An immense north facing wall of bare rock, ice, and perpetual snow, Ausangate is in the Cordillera Vilcanota fourteen degrees south latitude. It is flanked by a group of lesser peaks with Apu Jatunuma to the west and larger ones including Apu Santa Catalina, only slightly smaller than Ausangate to the east. Mirroring Ausangate, six miles to the northeast, is a series of impressive peaks, the Kallangate group, that rise knife-like, white and pristine through the clouds. Larger in overall mass with several peaks approaching 20,000 feet, these skyward citadels include Apus Collipa Ananta, Kallangate, Collquecruz, Chumpe, and as I am to learn much later, Apu Suryamana that is on no map.

Lying at the base of Ausangate is a glacier composed of elegantly shaped blue gray ice topped by a thick layer of compact snow whose runoff forms a lake that spills into a river that runs across quartz embedded stones. It flows north to join the Pichimuromayu River that eventually becomes the Mapacho River at Tinki, the community closest to Ausangate. More a cluster of small crooked buildings and open-fronted market stalls than a town, at Tinki the river continues northwest towards the community of Ocongate, where is splits in two. Gathering other streams in its course, the

Chapter Three: The Thin Edge of Silence

Mapacho flashes down from the Andes to join the Paucartambo River that runs East of the Sacred Valley towards Machu Picchu, and beyond into the Amazon, the mother of all rivers.

Across the river at Tinki and to the northeast, is a line of impressive snow-covered mountains surrounding the shrine of *Qoyllur Rit'i* with Apus Q'ollqepunku and Sinakara guarding to the left and right of the glacier. Every fall—May and June below the equator—and just after the full moon and before the winter solstice, the festival of Qoyllur Rit'i takes place in a high valley immediately below the glacier. The festival, the largest annual event in the Andes, is dedicated to perpetual snow and ice, the mantel of the Apus, the source of life-giving water, and attracts tens of thousands of pilgrims from Peru and Bolivia. Non-stop revelry goes on twenty-four hours over several days. The festival is followed by a nocturnal procession to witness sunrise at Tayankani, near Ocongate. *Ukukus,* men dressed as bears, venerate the spirit of ice with ritual dancing. To culminate the pageantry, the bear men carry blocks of the glacial ice on their backs to the site of the former Inkan temple of *Wiraqocha* in Cusco, now the central Cathedral, a distance of several days walk on foot from the mother glacier at Apu Qoyllur Rit'i. The Inkan rite of carrying blocks of ice to the temple coincides with the Catholic feast day of Corpus Christi, but it is *Illa Tesqi Wiraqocha,* the god of creation, that traditional Quechuas venerate.

The timing of our journey, overlapping with Qoyllur Rit'i and just before Corpus Christi, is unplanned, occurring in the same inexplicable way that has characterized my time with Sebastian. Over the years we have worked together, I've come to accept our way of journeying as part of the mystery of the Andes, the endless Peruvian enigma to which I am rooted, sometimes mired, most often uplifted.

Ten days later, we approach the mountain when the moon is rising three quarters full in the eastern sky. Our purpose is to make our way towards the great white massif looming in the distance to the south where over six to eight days we will perform ancient ceremonies that will precede my next initiation, the *Orcopuntakarpay.* The reason for this journey is to connect deeply with Apu Ausangate; to put meaning to my dream; to bring perspective to Sebastian's dilemma; and to further my quest to discover the secret of the Andes.

~

My initial search for the secret of the Andes began in 1969. In 1996, I returned to Peru. My first ceremonial experiences with the Q'ero occurred in 2000, and after many rituals of reciprocity my first *karpay* took place in 2004 at a sacred lake deep in the wilderness of Q'ero territory. Since then I have attended over one hundred despachos, ceremonies of reciprocity, and experienced many karpays, shamanic initiations, in the mountains around Cusco and other regions of the Peruvian and Bolivian Andes. My first initiation into the Q'ero shamanic way of knowledge, the *aynikarpay,* awakening to the path of Ayni, was unique because of the remoteness of the location and the stark beauty of the landscape, and because Sebastian and I, along with his wife Filipa, were the only people in a vast space of wilderness, our mutual language, silence.

Q'ero initiation ceremonies, karpays, typically take place at noon in a sacred setting in nature, the results quickening the initiate's consciousness. The teachings that follow provide the framework for the cultivation of Ayni, the awakening of the principle of reciprocity and universal responsibility. It facilitates reverence, and engenders respect. This initiation, however, is different. Parts will take place at midday, but because it is to engage the great Apu, part of it is to take place at night. It is only in the darkest, inner places of the earth, within caves at night, that we can reach deep enough to encounter the humbling power of non-ordinary reality.

A hybrid word, *Orco* means mountain in Quechua, and *punta* is a Spanish word signifying "the point." In sacred runasimi, it is *orcokaha,* from *kahaturpay,* to converse directly with the Apu. In Quechua, words are can run together when spoken. Therefore, the Orcopuntakarpay is an initiation ceremony to enlist the Apu to become one's personal ally.

Though traditionally the Orcopuntakarpay is restricted to the first three days in August, according to Sebastian's interpretation, my dream informed him that it is time for a new level of understanding requiring a powerful karpay to quicken shamanic consciousness. The Q'ero are flexible about rules, and he is certain that though outside traditional timing we have a legitimate purpose for proceeding with this ceremony. However, because we are operating independent of the rules, every step of the process must be perfect, each part evaluated carefully before the next can take place. Explicit and implicit approval from the Apu and awkikuna, the nature spirits of the area, must occur each step of the way. To sharpen the connection between dream and consciousness, the first part of the initiation entails exacting cleansing rituals. The second part takes place at night, under the full moon, involving elaborate ceremonies. The third phase of the initiation, if all the signs are in alignment, takes place at noon in the presence of the Apu.

My vision in Cusco and the rainbow that followed the disappearance of Suryamana, was the confirmation needed to journey to Apu Ausangate, even if not within the constrains of traditional timing. It is here, in the ice and snows near 20,000 feet that the wilderness will be our temple and the mountain the teacher.

∼

For this journey, we leave Cusco in a hired minivan and drive south. Since my last trip to this area, the road has been paved, but it is as sinuous as before, twisting back and forth, up and down valleys, and over mountains. We stop for supplies and lunch on huge bowls of lamb stew in the market place in Urcos, a town of tightly packed buildings, a pleasant plaza, with a small lake at the outskirts where the Inka Huascar is said to have plunged golden objects to hide them from Spanish greed. From there we drive past Ocongate, the southern gateway to Q'ero territory and twenty-five kilometers before Manuallane, the beginning of the eight-kilometer uphill trek to Qoyllur Rit'i, and finally along a dusty road to Tinki at 12,188 feet, the village closest to Ausangate.

Tinki is the site of a former Spanish hacienda, now a small

bustling market center for the local Quechua alpaca herdsmen and potato growers of the region around Ausangate. The village consists of a cluster of homes and a half dozen open-front shops, numerous makeshift stalls, and an outdoor market spilling over into the dirt street that runs through the town's center, colorful ponchos spread on the ground laden with the staples of mountain life, mostly potatoes of every variety. You could pass through Tinki in the space of one breath if it weren't for the fact that it was the end of the road.

Before we start our journey on foot to Ausangate, we buy *canasa,* pure cane alcohol, and *chica* made from corn to use as offerings. Sebastian visits local Quechua elders to request permission to perform ceremonies of reciprocity on their mountain. I present them with gifts of coca leaves, and Sebastian explains our mission. Only after receiving approval from these elders does he feel we are ready to depart.

We make our way through the village, weaving past scattered homesteads, simple adobe huts, and then an open field rimed with stonewalls. Along the alpaca trail, local Quechua women are working in a field harvesting potatoes. We stop to chat and they share *papawatya,* native potatoes roasted in hot coals underground. Sebastian talks with them in a soft voice, offering advice on healing a sick child and revitalizing a barren field. I watch the sun, holding steady overhead but soon to dip down the threshold of heaven. Around us are long rolling hills dotted with cream-colored alpaca, and beyond there is only sky and mountain.

~

Ausangate rises before us to the south, overwhelming the skyline, luminous against a cloudless sky. Sebastian and I press forward along a dry creek bed filled with stones, some the size of large melons, slowing our progress. My head is bowed; my pack heavy, my breathing hard and long, my eyes on the ground. From time to time I look up, careful not to sprain an ankle on loose stones, and take in the long view of the landscape. The sky, graying in the east behind the mountain, suggests snow, but to the west it is a translucent blue.

Chapter Three: The Thin Edge of Silence

In the foreground, sepia hills roll like waves, one after another rising steadily higher, upward towards the mountain that is heaven bound, earth connected. From where I stand, I can see rounded hills covered in soft brown grass and dotted with cream-colored alpacas like puffs of unwashed organic cotton, grazing so slowly that from a distance they appear not to move at all. The local Quechuas, who consider Apu Ausangate their protector, deem the Apu the source that bestows upon them abundant herds of alpacas. An essential link exists between Apu and human, and their alpacas. Without them humans cannot survive at this altitude. Alpacas provide wool for clothing and meat for nourishment. Tendons are used as twine and braded into rope, and bones are made into tools or crafted into flutes. A special relationship of reciprocity between human and animal is essential for the continuity of life. The Q'ero say, an alpaca first taught Ayni to humans.

Once in the high Andes, to survive a particularly brutal night of subzero temperatures, I took refuge among a herd of alpacas. With darkness upon me, the thermometer plunging, and completely exhausted, I prayed to the animals for help, and then collapsed on the ground and fell asleep on my poncho. When I woke, the alpacas had formed a circle around me, tightly packed together to preserve heat, and by doing so kept me alive. To this day, I am indebted to these beautiful animals with large brown eyes for having saved me.

Alpacas[10] and their close relative, llamas[11] that are used mainly as pack animals, are descended from the wild vicuña.[12] Domestication dates back more than 5,000 years. Alpacas graze up to 16,500 feet; but we will go higher where there are no trees or shrubs, and with little grass for grazing, no alpaca ventures to such heights.

The day is clear and from our distance of about twelve miles from the base of Ausangate, the entire Cordillera Vilcanota range is visible. The largest of a group of five mountains, Apu Ausangate is the centerpiece of a cluster of peaks that together form a massif of snow and ice. Around its base, gigantic stone outcroppings rise up the dark blue color of night. It is a full day's walk, or more, depending on weather and how skilled one is at covering distances at high altitude. Towards the northeast is another almost identically shaped, though somewhat smaller massif. The largest of this group is Collpa Anata, with Kallangate rising to the left, and behind them looms Collquecruz.

We continue along the creek bed, which in places becomes a stream where water seeps through the ground, turns to rivulets that flow down hill towards the stream that runs across the middle of a broad expanse of altiplano turf. Fingers of water run between the turf making them spongy and wet. Sebastian's sandals strapped to bare feet hardened by a lifetime of trudging through snow and over stones, handle the water well, but my expensive hiking boots become wet and heavy. At this altitude, lightness is advantageous; heaviness is not only a burden, but also a liability. He notices my discomfort and goes to higher, drier ground. I change to trekking sandals and drape my boots over my pack, which dry quickly in the intense sun and dry Andean air.

The sun, a brilliant yellow sphere, settles midway between the zenith and the crest of a battery of sepia hills to our right, the farthest northwest it will go before disappearing behind the mountain range. Within hours it will be much colder, with temperatures descending fast after sunset and dropping below freezing during the night. On these trips with Sebastian, I never carry a watch or thermometer, or altimeter. Date and day fall away, and I lose sense of linear time, and enter the circular world of timeless, measureless nature.

It is past noon and we have eaten little today. I become hungry and drift into daydreaming of roasted potatoes. There are at least six different flavors from the inner part nearest the crisp outer skin to the whitest part at the potato's core.

Earlier, we nourished ourselves with *papawatya,* potatoes roasted in the earth. They are made by building a fire, traditionally with desiccated alpaca dung since no trees grow this high, and tending it until there are sufficient hot coals, a job typically done by children. Then dozens of potatoes are thrown on the coals and covered with chunks of dirt and clay. In about an hour, the result is tender and nutritious baked potatoes, crisp on the outside with sweet white flesh inside that dissolves in your mouth and warms the stomach. To eat them takes skill. First the crisp outer skin is peeled off with your fingernails. This reveals the inner carbohydrate core, white and rich in nutrients. We eat these plain without salt, oil, or butter. Andean native potatoes provide energy for the endurance needed at high altitude and unlike commercial potatoes these heritage varieties, of which there are more than 4,000 in the Andes, are smaller than an egg but rich in trace minerals and vitamins.

Papas, the word for potato in Quechua, have specific names for each variation and preparation like the freeze-dried *ch'uño*[13] used to make a creamy soup. Boiling is the typical way to cook potatoes and is called *papawayk'u*. The method of baking underground is called *watya,* and roasted potatoes are papawatya. Cultivation dates back more than 8,000 years, and this staple of the Andes is so revered that planting is linked to celestial events related to the Pleiades constellation, and the names of lunar months correspond to the planting and harvesting of potatoes.

The near complete absence of humidity is dehydrating and thinking of the potatoes makes me thirsty. Pure water tastes sweet, not the chemical sweetness of sugar, but of the sustaining sweetness of the earth. Water's crystalline transparency is more brilliant than diamond, and where there is none, as precious. Without water, plants cannot grow. Animals cannot reproduce, and people do not thrive. Fresh mountain water is liquid air. The two, air and water, are the basic elements of life. For traditional Andean people, the third element is earth, and the essential ingredient between the human and the Apu is coca. Today, we share all three: potato, water, and coca, which will be our main fare for this journey.

Though there is water pooling from the ground, I am careful not to drink it as the icy temperature can cause hypothermia. There is also the possibility of giardiasis[14] and other common protozoan intestinal infections that cause abdominal bloating, pain, and diarrhea. These mountain streams once ran clean and one could drink freely, but things are different now. It is wise to be careful, and even in these remote mountain regions we boil our water.

We move along a narrow muddy trail that soon fades and becomes an alpaca path, and then disappears entirely. Stumbling on a loose stone snaps me out of my reverie. I think to myself: So this is the state I've come to, where small plain potatoes and pure water, followed by chewing coca leaves, is more than enough.

~

The going now is easier as we walk over hillsides covered in low grass, the ground firm under foot. However, Sebastian is relentless and we soon climb steadily higher. Cusco at 10,800 feet is within the high altitude zone of 5,000 to 11,500 feet. Tinki at 12,188 is considered very high altitude. The mountaineer's rule is to ascend no more than 1,000 feet per day. We have already gone more than that today, and will go higher. In the coming days, we will climb to an altitude over 19,000 feet and remain there for days.

The way is treacherous. I gasp for air, and keep alert for signs of altitude sickness. I must avoid sunburn during the day and frostbite at night. But no matter what the hardship–the journey with Sebastian is worth the discomfort.

The first two days are hard on feet and joints, even painful. But by the end of the journey, I will be stronger. I resolve to keep my old enemies, back and joint pain, at a distance. After more than a decade in the Andes, I am better prepared for this journey, and not overly concerned about the physical hardship. High mountain wilderness treks have many physical risks, but self-doubt and fear are the foes now. One must always remember that high altitude can kill. Yet the mind exaggerates the dangers, imaginary catastrophes loom large. Anxiety and fear, if not controlled, can turn to panic.

What am I doing here? How far will we go this time? What will we encounter? I know the answers.

I am here because we have prepared for this journey for more than a decade. We will go as far as we can. I await this initiation. I am ready to listen and learn what the great Apu may teach. Anxiety will not rule. I will put worry aside. I will allow munay to enter my

Chapter Three: The Thin Edge of Silence

heart and mind. I will see beauty around me. Where beauty exists, there is no fear.

Sebastian turns around, as if hearing my thoughts. Our eyes meet and though he has concerns too, his eyes glisten in the sun, radiate life, and I am exhilarated.

I look up. All is blue. The mountain fills the horizon, white. For the moment, everything is right in the world. The creator's hand is here, and she is beautiful.

"Hatunmunaycha," Sebastian cries out. "Great beauty."

"*Munaycha*," I echo back. It is indeed a wonderful day and we are surrounded by beauty.

～

The Q'ero are a quiet people. In all my journeys with them, there is little discussion; decisions are made deftly, comments are short and appropriate. Voices are soft and low. But when at rest or when finding a rhythm while walking, Sebastian can become talkative, his words no louder than footsteps, and even those muffled by the earflaps of the Andean knitted caps we wear, mine a wine red filled with yellow and blue.

An Andean Lapwing[15] bursts raucously a few yards to our left then settles down only to fly up again and circle this time with three other anxious birds, their gray and white coloring striking against the auburn and sepia of the low grasses. Finding us non-threatening, they land; the instant their feet touch down running in grass up to their bellies, keeping pace with us, their heads bobbing up and down ready at a moment's notice to sound the alarm again, and if necessary, launch into flight.

"*Lequecho*," Sebastian says without turning around.

Noisy birds, but I find them entertaining companions when walking the high Andean valleys. Every now and then, they look to see where we are going, fly up, then land and starting running again, keeping pace with us, all the while screeching as if we were devils. Once they find us harmless and we pass from their territory, tiring of our presence, they return to their own preoccupations of pecking the dirt for insects and furiously running along the ground.

We have been climbing steadily for hours. The air is thinning and noticeably colder the higher we go, and the walking gets slower. But we make steady progress, even though I stop from time to time to take photographs and make notes. However, I know that we have much ground to cover before making camp, and from here we will have to keep a steady pace, so re-pack my cameras and notebooks, put aside hopes to capture memories and insights, to climb ever upward towards Ausangate.

~

Stars appear and the darkening sky transforms the color of the stones to indigo. Clouds come fast from the southeast and form around the base of the mountain, filling in the valleys between the hills white. A wind picks, up blowing off the snow and ice hitting cold at the bare spots around my wrists and neck. Sebastian signals to descend to the right and we move off the high ground, out of the direct wind, and weave our way east into a pocket protected by large stone outcroppings.

To the west is a wide valley running from a point below the glacier at the foot of the mountain onto a flat plain dotted with small shallow ponds and a river weaves through the center. On both sides of the river on higher ground are scattered five adobe one-room huts thatched with grass and surrounded by stone corrals. Beige alpacas with a few brown and black ones graze nearby while others on the neighboring hills slowly make their way back to the safety of the corrals for the night. The slow descent of equatorial twilight comes early, as June is the beginning of winter in the Southern Hemisphere, and though daylight and nighttime are an equal twelve hours all year, there are seasonal changes in the atmosphere that make the approach of night seem slower.

A blinding white sun glides down the sky toward earth. Ahead, still a full day's walk, the Ausangate massif and surrounding peaks, which the Quechua consider relatives of the main mountain, spread wider and higher. It's been cloudless all day, but now gray clouds materialize around its base; dense vapor expanding fast up the slopes and pouring down the valley towards us like giant phantasms. The setting sun illuminates the peaks drenching them with pink and gold.

There is only my boots against stone. The moment is tangible; there is only here. There is only myself upon the earth, in the now. The mountain is alive.

~

We arrive at a hollow protected on three sides by tightly packed hills where several stone monoliths stand sentinel as if guarding the opening to the south, the direction of Ausangate. In the center is a stone corral used for protecting alpacas against puma attacks and this makes for a break against the sharp Andean wind, which blows constantly except for moments when there is a sudden pause, as if Pachamama inhaled deeply and then held her breath.

I sit down and look at the mountain. My breathing is shallower at this altitude, but the pure air energizes, and as I exhale, the wind stirs.

The sun, immense and round, hovering just above the western hills, casts long shadows that reach deep into the valleys. The contrast between yellow sunlight and shadow on the hills brings a sense of longing for the passing day, but also a concern for the night ahead. For the moment, the wind, buffered by the hills and rocks, appears calm but Sebastian keeps low and I find out why when I stand and the wind is strong at my shoulders and bites my neck. Soon the temperature will plummet. With each passing hour it will grow colder until it is well below freezing. For now, what remains of the day is on the edge of glorious.

Perhaps it's the altitude, which alters normal consciousness, making it more rarified, but I feel an inner shift, a sense of wholeness. Clouds suddenly take on shapes that carry new meaning. Words form in my head as if the clouds talk to me like friends, welcoming me to the mountain, affirming that this is a good journey.

A few alpaca linger nearby, most having moved on to safer

bedding places in the valley below, look at me with great knowing eyes, quiet in their methodical way of working their teeth in the grass, capturing the last minutes of sun before twilight. As they stare, I believe they are wishing me what is right on my journey to Ausangate. The stones contain their own wisdom, silent witnesses of everything and everyone that has passed here for thousands of years. Perhaps they have something to say. I pick up a fist-sized stone, put it to my ear like one would a seashell. I listen to its whispering; the earth stirs in this stone, then put it back in its place on the ground.

∼

This is the last "undemanding" place before the ascent to the mountain. But momentary ease generates great doubt. If this journey is not for me, now is the time to decide for tomorrow there will be no turning back. I remind myself that I have already made my decision, there is only going forward. A thin edge of silence is all that separates the mountain from my intent. The threshold of *becoming* to the purity of *being* hovers before me.

As quickly as it comes, the insight into what is true and good and real vanishes and I am left with mundane thoughts. My cameras require cleaning and protection, notebooks need unpacking, and bedding needs readying. Water needs to be set to boil on the propane stove, and potatoes peeled and added for soup. But before attending to these details, I pause for a moment savoring the last taste of day. Sebastian sits on his poncho, still and reflective, eyes closed, stoic and resolute. Then, he looks at me, his dark eyes mirroring the setting sun, and in the unspoken moment of shared places we are one in munay.

"Munaycha," he says. "Beauty is all around."

To enter the silence of the Apu, not just the geological silence of stone and ice, requires sacrifice. He will leave behind tribal history and personal future, traditional Q'ero and modern Peruvian, ancient and permanent, new and transient. Trapped between a harsh present and an unknown tomorrow, Sebastian's world is in flux; carrying with it is the possibility of rapid cultural unraveling. The historical part,

Chapter Three: The Thin Edge of Silence

his pre-Inkan ancestry, channels a deep connection to Pachamama through Ayni that is both message and responsibility. His present is the burden of poverty, lack of education, and racial discrimination. Sebastian's dilemma is to find a way to keep it whole, to retain the cultural and spiritual essence of his people, and yet be resilient in the face of rapid change. After generations of resistance, he must yield to acculturation into a system that the Q'ero did not create, or choose, a system that shocks and shames as it spreads its spiritual poverty and dysfunction across the planet.

I attempt to release the last grip of my Western mind with its linear way of learning. I let go of dualism and premeditated thinking, loosen the knots of opinions, and instead hold to stillness, the unexpected. Sebastian and I have come to this turning point together, to this mountain, Ausangate, and I will leave regrets and past failures behind, even if only to pick them up later when we return. For now, the anxieties of what will happen tomorrow or next week or the following year are of no consequence above 19,000 feet. To survive and come back whole is no longer enough. To reach the next level, I must surrender to the Apu. I must release myself to something larger than one lifetime, something more mystical than the literalness of a mountain.

As the sun goes down behind the hills, we huddle inside the stone corral, braced against a wind coming cold off the glacier, bearing down at us between the hills funneling through the valley as if to inform us of what is to come.

The snows of Ausangate rise above the hills. Clouds form around its base, climbing upward along the slopes. Soon the entire massif, under which snow will fall in the night, will drift into cold, clean, slumber. Tomorrow and over the next several days, we will see if the mountain allows us to come close, or if it will rain cold and send sharp granules of hail on us. For the moment, the upper most peak points high above the clouds, into the sky, a white ember reflecting the ray of the sun, setting the snow ablaze.

~

Sebastian and I sit under a three quarter moon rising incandescent behind Ausangate. Our journey falls between Andean autumn and winter, a month after the rainy season and well before the intense cold immaculate skies of winter. We are simply here together, journeying to Ausangate. Wrapped in his poncho, Sebastian talks softly in Quechua while clouds, visible in the intense moonlight, drift off the mountain down the valley. He heats water that takes longer to reach a boil at high altitude, and adds a few slices of carrots and onion, and lots of potatoes. Finally our dinner is done, and we spoon mouthfuls of hot broth and boiled potatoes to warm us from the inside. When finished eating and plates put aside to wash in the morning, Sebastian brings out coca leaves and spreads them on an uncuño. We gather tight around the sacred leaves, select the most perfectly shaped ones, and offer each other k'intus, three leaves symbolic of the grand spheres of existence and the three levels of life.

With a k'intu clasped lightly between my first three fingers, touched to heart and then to lips, I perform the phukuyr'tti, the ritual mingling of breath with the great respiratory cycle of Pachamama, offering one's existence to the greater life around us, whispering a prayer to Apu Ausangate: "Great being—Apu Ausangate, I am here under the sky and moon; here in your presence, surrounded by the great beauty you have created, sitting, waiting."

For the next hour, we carefully select more coca, separating the most perfectly shaped leaves from the common ones, arrange them in groups of three, pointed and perfect, the largest leaf in the center symmetrically fanned, and present more k'intus to each other. Pray more. Chew methodically. Be careful not to over grind the leaves, packing large wads of masticated leaf between teeth and gum, to better extract the essence of coca.

Uramama, "mother coca," the respectful way of addressing the coca plant in sacred runasimi, *kuka* in common Quechua, and coca in Spanish and English, is held in Q'ero tradition as the "bridge" between humans and the mountain spirits, the Apus. Every meeting and every teaching begins with the ritual sharing of coca leaves. Before embarking on a journey, before making important decisions and imparting knowledge, coca leaves are shared for the purpose of tuning to the spirit of the Apus. An ancient consensus of equals, each person accepting the interdependence of nature and man, the joining of all things that live in cooperative harmony upon the great earth mother, embedded in the Milky Way they call *Mayu,* brushed across the heavens suspended in the cosmos. The Q'ero allow for one plant as essential and sacred—coca. And it is this leaf that binds hearts and mind: the material, mortal mind with the eternal spiritual heart.

Fed and warm, we are in good spirits, and pass more k'intus as we offer prayers to Pachamama and the Apus, to good health and fortune, and then speak encouraging words about the journey ahead. Sebastian talks gently wishing me a good journey; and receiving his k'intu, I thank him, and offer up the spirit of the coca leaves to the Apus, naming them one by one, acknowledging our interdependent relationship to Pachamama, the energy that provides life to all things.

Sebastian lights *palo santo,*[16] "holy tree," a naturally aromatic wood native to Peru in the same family as frankincense and myrrh. The highly combustible resin flames bright in the clay receptacle we bought along, making strong clouds of thick, fragrant smoke and we're enveloped in the sweet smell, which lightens my mood while the effects of the coca lessen the cold. The bond of men in the wilderness, native Quechua and white American, tightens.

I take *mapacho* cigars out of my pack, wild Amazonian tobacco[17] that I brought with me from the rainforest and produce two, one for each of us. Before lighting them, and as taught by my Shipibo shaman mentors in the upper Amazon, I blow three times into the cluster of mapachos, passing my breath, life force, into each one.

Sebastian takes his from my fingers, the Q'ero rarely smoke tobacco but welcome these gifts of the forest, says: "Compadre Santiago, I thank you and offer gratitude to Pachamama for this tobacco."

I light our mapachos, the ember glowing in the night, and inhale. The effect of the tobacco is calming and refreshing, and opens my lungs. We blow smoke, avoiding inhaling too much because this type of tobacco is very strong and can cause severe dizziness and even hallucinations. This effect is naturally accentuated at high altitude. We make our offering to the mountain and the moon, *Mamakilla*, soon to reach full, whispering personal prayers of gratefulness and benediction. I am thankful to be here with Sebastian, my closest friend in the world, nearing the sacred mountain, entering the silence of being, present in this icy, star-filled night.

"Munaycha," Sebastian says softly.

We are quiet as we finish our mapachos. The scent of wild tobacco blends with the aromatic incense from the palo santo, which when combined with the clarity of coca creates a mild euphoria, and despite the cold there is a lightening of the load, the accumulated pressure of days of preparation for the journey, the years of impatient waiting for this journey, and the greater burdens of life that we carry, without even knowing it, soften and dissolve in the thin air.

"Santiago," he opens the conversation that I know was coming, "I would like to speak."

"Hai," I answer. "I am listening."

A long silence follows as we finish the last of our mapachos, the final embers glowing red at the tip, smoke curling upward towards the mountain and the moon. When we finish, I crush what remains of the tobacco. It turns to powder between my fingers and I sprinkle it along with a cluster of six k'intus on a small stone altar Sebastian made at the side of the corral, putting a rock on top to prevent the leaves from blowing away.

Returning to my place next to Sebastian, I sit cross-legged and turn inward, intimate with moon and stars. When we are comfortable and all is quiet, he begins in a mixture of Spanish and Quechua. Every so often, he pauses, waiting patiently to be sure my understanding is sufficient, as utmost certainty, a trademark characteristic of Q'ero shamanism, is essential during preparation for advanced karpays.

"You have been among us for twelve years," Sebastian begins.

Chapter Three: The Thin Edge of Silence

"These have been long, slow years but we have made steady progress."

"It has been so slow, papa, and for that I am sorry."

"This is as it should be," he answers reassuringly, calming my doubts; then selecting his words carefully, goes on: "The Apus guide the process. Know this. When change comes too fast, it can turn to confusion. It takes time for plants to grow from the earth. Like steady growth produces a strong tree, wisdom comes slowly."

His tone is soft and metered, and he pauses often, allowing space for clarity to come to his lesson. Should the Apu listen, each word must ring true.

"We are human and bound to make mistakes along the way. When things progress slowly," Sebastian continues, "there is time to adapt to mishaps. When we take the time to consider our lessons, we learn from our mistakes. Compadre, we suffer our way to wisdom."

I had been feeling miserable because of how long my work in Peru was taking, how little money I was able to raise to house and feed the Q'ero, how they had to suffer the long arduous and dangerous journey back and forth from their home village in the heights of Hatun Q'ero to Cusco. And the psychological toll and heavy expense of traveling back and forth to Peru—all were stressful and hard on my personal and professional life. Sebastian's words put my heart at ease, and for the moment, the mental agony of unfulfilled expectations stilled enough for me to truly listen.

"We are about to do some thing that has not been done for a long time. Even I have only participated one other time in this powerful ceremony. Many come to Cusco looking for answers outside themselves. They believe the Q'ero have magical powers to heal them and quick ways to turn them into shamans. But they have not done the work. This path requires great sacrifice. The quick method is not our way. You know this well because you live with us. You plant potatoes with us and eat the food of the earth, watch our children grow, feed our people when hungry, tend to us when we are sick, and listen to our hopes for a better life. You see with your own eyes. Your heart is open. You work side-by-side with us to make a better future."

Sebastian pauses. I wait for him to continue.

"We are your spiritual family and your guides and interpreters of Pachamama's teachings. This is the way of the Q'ero. Our knowledge is passed down, generation upon generation, from a time before the Inkas. The original knowledge came to us from Pachamama and to our pakuqs directly from the Apus. We are sharing all of this with you. This is what makes it a living tradition. Each generation renews itself by direct contact with the spiritual energy of Pachamama and the wisdom of the Apus."

"Hai." I nod in agreement.

After another pause, he begins again: "In previous generations it was different. During my father's time things began to change. Before, the Apus sought the shaman, but now the shaman has to go to the Apu."

I sense where the lesson is going, but I have no idea where it will end up. Like the letting go that occurs when falling into a deep sleep, and that I suspect also must come when dying or when the ego lets go on the threshold of spiritual realization, wisdom does not come by willing it into existence. Wisdom comes in its own time. Only when you find release from the life-and-death grip of the ego can you learn from the Apu.

But even when you reach the portal, the door is often closed and locked. Like the stories of the Zen aspirant who finally arrives at the temple after a long arduous journey and is turned away, the only predictable thing is that it will be difficult coming and going. The guardians of the Apu are fear and dread. At this juncture in my shamanic training, there can be no more doubts, no more concerns over past decisions. For the duration of the journey, all belief and expectations are put aside. Buried. It is what it is. Not what I imagine it to be. Worries will wait. So will expectations. This is not a journey to enlightenment. It is to step beyond fear, to become as clear as the sky.

"Coming to the Apu in this way and sharing your journey with us is good," he continues as if answering my thoughts. "Your patience in not going to Ausangate until you were called is a sign to the Apu that you know how to wait. The question now is how will you respond if the Apu speaks. You are taking on an immense responsibility. I will help by preparing the way, but only you can take the final step; only you will know when that time comes to enter the mystery."

A master weaver of an ancient oral tradition, Sebastian spins threads of wisdom, offers advice, and provides encouragement. In ancient times, he tells me, when wise men and empathic women had tranquil minds and quiet hearts, and listened deeply to nature, the message of Pachamama and the Apus, and Sachamama—the gigantic master teaching serpent of the forest—was self-evident. With mental clarity and emotional dexterity, he tightens the truly important points, sifts the merely interesting from the necessary and vital, and weaves words on the loom of earth-based wisdom. As the shuttle of consciousness moves back and forth repetitiously, with each pass he adds finely spun threads of pure knowledge on how to sustain human culture, how to live righteously in harmony with all life.

Over the years I worked with him, no matter where he started, the underlying tone is the same. Like the design of their ponchos, the fabric of teaching bears an identical pattern, universal and simple, and comes back to a core understanding, one inalienable truth, a single principle: a hundred and one insights become a single point of light—Ayni.

In Cusco, it is understood as reciprocity *(reciprocidad)* or appreciation *(agradecimiento)*. But, I have come to learn that Ayni is considerably more. It is better understood as reciprocity *and* responsibility.

The Q'ero employ Ayni in relationship with Pachamama and the Apus. They show their appreciation for the gifts of the earth, itself the highest form of reciprocity, and the protection of the Apus through ceremonial offerings, despachos. There is the expectation that if offered with the right attitude of heart, good fortune will result. At its purest level, despachos are done for intrinsic reasons— the act alone is the reward.

Sebastian teaches through his example and by oral tradition that there is one fundamental ethic that guides his people, the same one they have followed over the millennia. The secret of the Andes is simple. Like a golden compass, there is one principle—Ayni. In all my interactions, discussions, and experiences with the Q'ero, I found this to be the common theme. There are several rules of balanced living, but Ayni guides them all.

He emphasizes that every journey, including the personal and collective, requires a guiding star, a true point in the heavens by which to navigate. A compass that always points north. That true point, Ayni, is the fundamental message of the Q'ero, the real secret of the Andes.

As the moon rises higher, he talks on about Ayni.

"Yesterday, I helped you. Today, we work together. Tomorrow, you help me."

For the hundredth time, Sebastian teaches me the fundamentals; repetition, like the turning of a Tibetan prayer wheel, is required until it becomes a personal mantra.

"This is every day Ayni," he says. "Without it, society doesn't stick together. When we follow Ayni, there is balance. But, if we neglect to practice Ayni in our daily life and ignore the cycles of nature, things fall apart. Pachamama is forgotten. Things become imbalanced. We lose our way."

The practice of Ayni is called *aynikawsay*. In daily life, Ayni is amiability, appreciation, and altruism. In the community, it manifests as cooperation and mutual assistance. For the individual, it is reciprocity, respect; and, for the pakuq it is reverence and remembrance. In its highest form, it is universal responsibility.

According to the Q'ero, Ayni is the most useful and profoundly noble lesson that we will learn in life. It is the flow of energy co-created by the interchange of loving kindness, knowledge, and the fruits of one's labor—*munay, yachay, llank'ay*—the three fundamental principles of the Andean way. Of the three, munay is the closest to Ayni. One can return to the state of pure love and beauty, the essence of munay, through the selfless practice of Ayni, the way of being in the state of munay through Ayni—*Aynipimunaykawsay.*

Ayni is a universal principle as well as a practice among people, between humans and Pachamama, and between the pakuq and the living web of energy and pure intelligence the Q'ero call Apus. By practicing Ayni, one acknowledges that every thing is sacred and all things are related. Because it sustains and supports all life, Ayni requires conscious acknowledgement and willing participation in the connection between the human and the natural world. Therefore, Ayni requires of us remembrance. It instills reverence, fosters resilience, and it emphasizes universal responsibility *and* reciprocity.

Like a kind of spiritual gravity, Ayni holds things together; keeps things in their rightful place, and assures that our children will have the same, if not more, opportunities than we have. Ayni binds past and future through the present. During hard times, Ayni keeps things together. It reminds us of the responsibility we have, personal and planetary, to the dimension of our lives, familial and universal. It promotes sustainability and requires abiding resilience and healthy interdependence.

The guiding star of the Q'ero, Ayni is present in all aspects of their lives, and is symbolized in their textiles. For them, there is no more noble work than to practice Ayni.

"Ayni is the seed and the fruit. It connects the leaf to the branch, and the tree to the roots in the earth," Sebastian reminds me.

He says it is important to keep it simple, whole, and grounded in human values. Noble. In his homeland, his hut is open to everyone. Everyone is invited to dinner; everyone gets something to eat.

In its purest form, Ayni is a state of mind. When the mind is attuned to the principle of reciprocity it naturally promotes happiness for oneself and others, and the mind is at peace and the heart calm. Transformation, I am to soon learn, begins within one's self. But also it is our relationship to all other things. It does not come from outside.

Sebastian informs me that the pakuq nurtures a special form of Ayni with the Apus. In addition to this, the shaman adheres to the same ethical guidelines as everyone else. But he is held to a higher standard with others and with nature. The pakuq serves his family, the community, and Pachamama *and* the Apus.

I begin to understand Sebastian's dilemma with greater clarity. When we see ourselves as co-creators and act as co-producers of goods, wealth is shared, not hoarded. In the case of the Q'ero, wealth is based on successful potato farming and measured in numbers of alpacas. Among them, envy and greed, over consumption and accumulation are viewed as forms of evil. Unbalanced and ultimately destructive to others and one self, overly self interested behavior reaps what it sows: isolation and unhappiness. Unhealthy behavior leads to an unbalanced mind, a disturbed heart, and eventually an unhealthy body.

Sebastian's words are precise and measured, no doubt he has talked it over with his people for days before we left Cusco, likely longer, waiting for the right moment to address what needs to be said before we reach the mountain. There will be more teaching, but for tonight he is finished, and it is time to sleep.

∼

Stars come out one by one until the canopy of heaven is full of light. The moon, rising to the east, lights our camp. Clouds retreat to the mountain, guarding the Apu for the night. The rest of the sky is clear and the night stretches cold and drives us into our blankets.

Sebastian lies motionless, a stillness patterned on stones. His eyes, wide-open, gaze at the night sky. From under his covers, he continues to talk in Quechua, but I cannot understand everything; his voice soft and resonant, his primeval words lull me towards slumber.

After some time, he closes his eyes and opens his heart, and embraced by Pachamama, falls asleep.

With my head to the mountain, I release every expectation, drift in the silence of the Apus into a deep dreamless sleep.

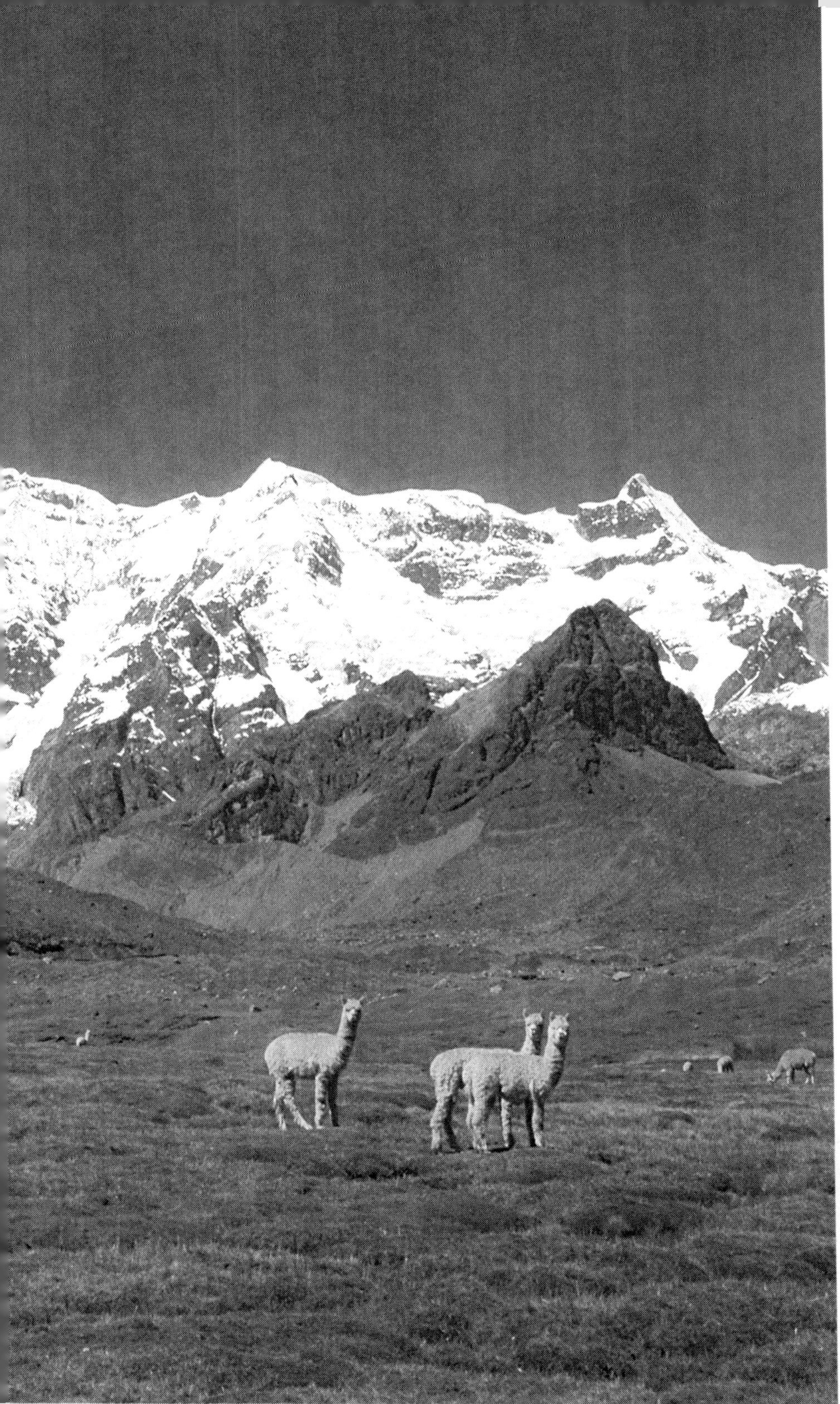

Previous page:

Alpacas in a high plain in front of northeast slope of Ausangate.

~ CHAPTER FOUR ~
# EARTH MOUNTAIN SKY

The moon has long gone into the west, leaving the midnight sky diamond bright. In the absence of moonlight, because of an illusion created by the thin air of equatorial high altitude, stars appear brighter and closer. There is an urgent quite, a silence falls. Stillness stalks. The wind calms, dies, the only movement is the slow traverse of stars.

I wake up cold. It is below freezing and ice is forming on the grass. I sleep in long underwear with a fleece cap on, and even zipped up in a down sleeping bag, I am uncomfortable. Every part of my body aches. Though not the quaking cold of higher altitudes, it is so shivery that I cannot get back to sleep.

Sebastian is awake too. From the warmth of his poncho and blankets, he extends an arm and points to the Southern Cross, *Huch'uy Chakana*, and then to other constellations, naming them one by one in Quechua.

"This is *Urkuchillay*, the little llama. This is *Yakumama*, the serpent. And this one is *Willka Wara*, our sacred star."

The Milky Way arches overhead. Our sun, Inti in Quechua, is but one of billions of stars in the spiral galaxy. The Chinese call the Milky Way the "silver river." The Spanish name it *El Camino de Santiago*, "The Way of St. James." Santiago is the patron saint of Cusco, and my namesake in Peru. The Q'ero, and their Inkan forefathers, know it as *Mayu,* the sacred river in which all souls swim. Masters of the seasonal rhythms of Mayu, the celestial river that flows across the sky until it joins the Southern Cross at its terminus, the Q'ero inherited an extensive applied astronomy from the Inkas. The Andean sacred star is Sirius, the brightest star in the night sky. Traditional Andean agriculture depends on a detailed knowledge of stars. The night sky is the Q'ero "clock" timing planting and harvesting.

"Santiago," Sebastian says softly, "we are the smallest of the small in the great body of Pachamama."

The Q'ero consider humans mere cells in the infinite body of the cosmic mother, Pachamama, which forms the visible and invisible universe. Though Pachamama is vast and we are infinitesimally small, even she is but one layer of existence in an even greater universal body where time and space coexist simultaneously; where every memory, every thought, every emotion is stored in one great field of cosmic intelligence.

In Sanskrit this cosmic field is called *Akasha,* the eternal source of all energy, the supreme source that creates and nourishes everything; all directions at once. Ervin Laszlo, the author of *Science and the Akashic Field,* called it the "heart of the cosmos, a Metaverse of super-dense energy, super-rich information field transcending cosmos and consciousness."[18] The Q'ero call it *Pacha.*

According to the Q'ero worldview, every aspect of life is interwoven in one seamless tapestry of cosmic order. The Earth is the visible realm of Pachamama and therefore, everything in life is sacred. Our living planet is but one of the many manifestations of Pachamama. The physical earth, *la tierra* in Spanish, is called *allpa* in Quechua, and is our biosphere, the envelope of life. Pachamama in the greater sense is the divine feminine, the creative energy of the universe. We are part of a whole from the earth's core to the biosphere, upward to the heavens as one interconnected web of life and energy. Plants in their sprouting, growing, and ripening; animals in their fertility cycles, weather patterns, and the transit of stars in the night sky are all part of this cosmic web of intelligent, living, energy.

For the Q'ero, these heavenly connections are interlinked and overlap the human sphere. Even human logic, as well as emotion and the unpredictability of human behavior, are interconnected parts of one universal whole. From the calligraphy of clouds to bird song in the trees, the hum of dragonflies, humans laboring in the fields, the stars overhead, all one hive of being and becoming.

This encompassing worldview takes in everything terrestrial and celestial with humans playing an integral role between the microcosmic world and the macrocosm. Ever conscious of their place between heaven and earth, the Q'ero favor humility in their role as custodians of earth-based wisdom and spiritual knowledge. The Q'ero are integrated holistically, not as lords of the land, but as caretakers. To this day, they keep an ember of pre-Inkan earth-based wisdom burning in the Andean wilderness, a territory of beauty and violence where nature is majestic, and also extreme. Condors devour newborn alpacas. Pumas kill llamas. Humans, as the Q'ero remind us, regardless of where they live, are responsible to keep the balance of heaven and earth; to practice acts of reciprocity in order attune with Pachamama. Though not completely vegetarian, the Q'ero shun hunting for sport and even for food. They are agriculturalists and pastoralist, who eat fish, primarily mountain trout, and occasionally sacrifice a lamb or alpaca for meat, and they use every part of the animal so nothing is wasted.

To appreciate the concept of Pachamama and Ayni is to understand the Q'ero worldview, the Metaverse of the Inkas, *Pachakawsay,* the blending of time and life.

In reverse–*kawsaypacha*–means one's lifespan. This two-way, alternate current implies that we have to live on the planet as one human family, in good relations with all living things. In awe and reverence to the Metaverse around us, Pacha, and we are guided by one master principle—Ayni.

Pacha is the wholeness of life. Everywhere without being anywhere, Pacha is the entire living universe: energy and matter, visible and invisible, organic and inorganic, the mundane and the mystical, everything and nothing, the human and the divine. All that ever existed and will exist, and everything that could or could not exist are in the realm of Pacha.

For the Q'ero, Pachamama is the Universe: being and becoming, known and unknown, time-bound as well as transcendental. A cosmic being, the divine feminine, Pachamama is everything and nothing, simultaneously–the "mother" of all things.

When asked to describe her, a Q'ero shaman will answer with a pure and steady silence.

∼

Sebastian lies quiet and his regular breathing tells me he is asleep. He is genetically well adapted to high altitude, and is accustomed to harsh conditions. For him, sleep comes easily and goes deep. It is not the same for me; nights can be difficult at this altitude. It is hard for me to breathe, and lying down worsens the condition so sleep comes interrupted with gasping and sudden waking. As we go higher, my heart and lungs will work harder, the thin air is never enough, so sleeping is even more difficult. I am grateful, however, for tonight will be my last good rest. Eventually, I fall back asleep bundled in my alpaca poncho, good insulation against the freezing night.

∼

I wake up slow. Sebastian is already stirring, but not up yet. Ice is on the ground. It is not warm enough to get up. Wrapped in layers, we wait for the rising sun. We talk quietly, so as to not disturb the Apu, and make plans for the day's trek upward towards the mountain. Perhaps I should rename it *Cold Mountain* from the book by the Chinese Taoist poet, Han Shan. It will get well below freezing as we venture skyward, but Sebastian's concern is not for the cold or the altitude, but rather our *attitude* as we approach the mountain. So I stay warm in my cocoon thinking about the day ahead, listening to the soft guttural sound of Quechua interspersed with heavily accented Spanish. After a while, I fall back into a deep dreamless sleep.

∼

Chapter Four: Earth Mountain Sky

I waken to brilliant sunlight and a cloudless blue sky. A lacework of white ice, dazzling in the morning sun, covers the ground. The landscape glistens and the ice crackles under foot as I get up and move about. Sebastian, already up, is heating water for coca leaf tea, mate de coca, which has little of the consciousness-clarifying effects of the chewed leaves, but is warming and stimulating enough to energize the start of our day. In the dry air, dehydration comes quickly, and this altitude compounds it. The warm mate adds electrolytes, but it's also a strong diuretic and good for cleansing the kidneys and bladder. For best effect we make it strong, but I do not drink too much at one time, otherwise I will have to make frequent stops to urinate, and become more dehydrated. Little sips of very concentrated coca tea work best.

The propane stove I bought in Cusco spares us from using dried alpaca dung, which is the traditional way to make a fire in the Andes. On my other trips we did it the old way, but now, even with the blue flame of propane it still takes a long time to boil water.

During the night the clouds that had blanketed the mountain have dissolved, leaving Ausangate dressed in new snow, pure white against a sapphire sky. I shiver inside, as much from the morning cold as from apprehension for the day ahead: How high will we go? How cold will it get?

While the water boils, I walk to the top of the nearest hill. The landscape spreads out in all directions cloudless, immense, and unfathomable, snowcapped mountains forming a perimeter in the distance. In this air, visibility is more than forty miles. To the west is Apu Salkantay, near Machu Picchu, that forms the northern border of the sacred Cusco region, Apu Ausangate forming the southern border. To the right is Apu Veronica, north of the Sacred Valley, then Apus Pumahuanca, and Chicon, where the people of Urubamba stir at its base, and then Apus Pitusiray and Sawasiray. Further to the south is a cluster of mountains that form the border of Q'ero territory, Apus Qoyllur Rit'i and Sinakara. The legendary birthplace of the Q'ero, Apu Qollquepunkqo, stands at the border between cloud forests and the Andes.

We are some ways off from the next camp, but in Q'ero style we will cover three times the distance a typical trekking group would do in the same amount of time. Sebastian knows exactly how much energy to expend and how intensely we need to walk, at times run, to cover the ground necessary to camp before nightfall. There will be short rests, but no lunch. Along the way, he never drinks water. However, I will sip from the water bottle I brought along to ward off dehydration.

Andean people know that abundant fluids are necessary in the dry climate of the altiplano, but believe that though water is good for plants and animals, it is not healthy for people. Instead, they drink large quantities of fermented corn or quinoa called chica, potato soup, and herbal teas called mates. Sebastian, in accord with Q'ero tradition avoids drinking water, and cautions me to do the same.

He will go without fluid from after breakfast to dinner. I, on the other hand, dehydrate easy from an imperceptible evaporation of sweat. If I pant heavily, gasping air through my mouth in a futile attempt to charge my lungs with oxygen, it's worse. Mindful of his advice, I drink only in sips, as cold water drops the body's core temperature. There is an internal balance to maintain. The Q'ero are masters at this, but as a lowlander, I am handicapped.

There is also the difference of age. Sebastian is ten years younger than I am, and he is born to these mountains. I cannot go at his pace but keep up, metering my progress with brief rests stops. Though my sojourns in the high Andes have been many—and long enough for my blood to have more red cells and higher amounts of hemoglobin than ordinary, which allows my blood cells to carry more oxygen—I am disadvantaged genetically. Still, I am tempered to the journey and never fall far behind.

Though the sun has been up for over an hour, the ground is still frozen and the thin air biting. As we head out towards the mountain, breathing comes hard. I meter my respiration, adjust my pack, let my legs loosen to find their rhythm.

The pace takes over. It's less about strength, which is rigid and breakable, and more about flexibility, fluidity, and flow. It's about letting go, adapting without resistance. The mantra, as in all holy places, is to go silent. Allow the spirit of the land to measure my steps. Breathe. Walk. Breathe. Walk.

For this journey, I hoped to illuminate some aspect of Q'ero shamanism, but at this elevation, pushing past 16,000 feet, now my only desire is to put in a good showing. I have three rules. One: don't drop behind. Two: stay focused and alert. And three: keep hydrated. Break one and things get tough.

Sebastian has his rules too: get up and go, slow down when it gets higher, but do not stop until you arrive, and never get caught in the open at night. When about to cross very high passes, stop to rest for about one hour before summiting, however during the climb, no matter how steep, keep a steady pace upward, even if slow, advancing without stopping until reaching the top. Surrounded in beauty, acknowledge the Apus: make a small stone altar, place some coca leaves as an offering, play your reed flute, say a prayer; then start down the mountain with a good heart.

My head bowed, the dry grass meets my eyes and melts into a golden haze. When I look up, there are the mountains; unbearably beautiful, knife-edged fins layered in wind sculpted snow.

The way ahead is over immense rolling hills, one bigger and higher than the next. Some of the crests are dotted with cream-colored alpaca and always behind is the snow mass of Ausangate. There are no valleys and no ridges now, and the hard ground makes running a natural for Sebastian, but an effort for me. Even under a heavy load, he still finds energy to sprint.

Bad fitting shoes are the bane of high altitude trekking. Mine are of good quality and fit well, as I have learned the hard way with sores worn to the bone, blood in my shoes, and deep open wounds so painful that I could not walk for days and took weeks to heal. If my feet swell from the low pressure of high altitude, I will change them for trekking sandals, which Sebastian agrees is the only true footwear for high mountain travel.

My body is lean and hardened, but the first few days bring intense soreness of muscles and joints. The cold stiffens and it takes me some time to warm up to a comfortable pace. After three days, tendons and ligaments adapt, and body intelligence memorizes what must be done to survive. Contracting cold and swelling heat trains muscles and joints to work more efficiently. In time, ligaments become more flexible, resilient. I can walk days without tiring. It's this second day of arduous climbing, alternating between running and walking, however, that tests mind and body.

I plod on behind Sebastian. His calves are the size of melons that pulsate when he moves. Before starting off, he never warms up, never stretches out before or after these long marches. I've never seen him hobble on sore feet or complain of cramped legs.

Sebastian wears *ajutas,* simple sandals made of rubber from worn out tires. His weathered feet are toughened by a lifetime of rough walking in cold water, traversing over ice and snow, and jagged stones. Nothing deters him. In the old days, the Q'ero as well as other Quechuas wore sandals made from alpaca skin. The ones they wear now are cheap commercial versions, but nearly indestructible, and easy to repair with a rock and knife. Men and women, and children, wear ajutas in rain or sun, heat or cold, rocky terrain and when crossing icy streams, and in snow and sleet.

∼

Without picking up or slowing my pace, my eyes half closed, I traverse a landscape where in the morning our shadows followed to our right, then behind us, and are now to our left. Sebastian's expression is set firm, each footstep steady. The ascent laborious at times is now tediously slow as we pass beyond the rolling terrain of morning and into rougher rockier ground of the afternoon. Here rocks come loose and crumble noisily underfoot. Twelve-foot high boulders litter the landscape where the glacier dropped them when it receded, leaving hundreds of egg-shaped, ice-sculpted stones precariously balanced and ready to come loose at any moment.

We press on, ever upward, the mountain sometimes in view but at others, as we move through sharp crevices, hidden from sight. Concave valleys, smooth as the curve of a cup and absent in the morning are now seen over nearly every hill. On each rise we crest, the mountain reappears. Ausangate is grander and looms larger until it is an enormous presence that fills my field of vision.

I stand on a hilltop; my thoughts turn to nothingness. There is only mountain. Sebastian joins me and we lie down on our backs looking up at a transparent sky, immersed in the seamless beauty of things. Pure sky. Spirit mountain.

∼

We continue on, but go slower now, long past grazing alpacas, too high even for these hardy animals, and find ourselves at an elevation where there are no trees, no bushes—where even tuffs of grass are confined to sheltered places between large stones where the wind cannot tear them out. Soon there will be none at all. The terrain is rockier. Some are partially covered in thin lichens, but most are bare, too cold at night and too hot by day to support even simple forms of life. The loose gravel and sharp stones make for difficult footing. Huge boulders are scattered across our path, so we weave around them, slowly working our way upward.

For the last miles, we climb beside a stream purling over boulders into deep pools. Sebastian says there are no fish at these heights, even though the stream looks ideal for firm-fleshed, sweet tasting Andean trout. But any way, there will be no meat or flesh of any kind on this journey as such ceremonies require a strict diet of simple vegetarian food and coca leaves. At extreme altitude, appetite is almost non-existent, so this restricted diet is acceptable to me, and there is no limit on the amount you can consume. I've learned from the Q'ero that consuming volumes of hot liquids like potato soup, rich in antioxidants and electrolytes is essential. At high altitude, even if my appetite is suppressed, I spoon in as much as he does. Staying well hydrated helps thin the blood; lack of fluid does the opposite. Thinner blood gets oxygen and nutrients to body tissues faster than thick, sticky blood.

Equally important, we do not drink cold water even when thirsty. Drinking cold fluids or sucking on ice or snow reduces core body temperature and it also acts as a diuretic, so as urination increases, dehydration accelerates. At high altitude, profound changes take place in body fluid balance, blood becomes more concentrated, and the kidneys excrete more fluid, which increases the concentration of red blood cells. This counteracts edema, but as a result, you urinate more. Keeping warm, including the head is also important, one reason the Q'ero always wear the traditional knitted cap. A colder body temperature can lead to hypothermia, and the combination of dehydration and hypothermia can result in death.

Another symptom of altitude sickness is headache—a horrible combination of pressure and pounding. It feels as if one's head is held in a tight vice while being struck with a hammer; the pain from brain swelling is deep, piercing, and vision blurs. Sometimes, high altitude headaches are due to dehydration; other times it's the accumulation of fluid in the brain. Either condition can produce severe symptoms, often accompanied by nausea and extreme weakness, and incapacitating headaches. In its worst form, high-altitude cerebral edema occurs. This can cause mental confusion and emotional instability leading to irrational behavior, delusions, and hallucinations.

The effects of high-altitude hypoxia increase with age. My passion drives me to be here as it once did years ago. It is more than raw passion—I am called, I believe, to serve, and there are consequently risks when climbing high to hear the Apu speak. Over the years, I have tried unsuccessfully to convince myself that these journeys are dangerous, life threatening. In the mean time, between sojourns to the Andes, I grow older, and I tell myself: Next time, I'll do it differently. I won't bolt up the mountain. I'll savor a slow ascent and dally along the way, photograph more, talk longer with local Quechua, write notes with greater precision. Already the cold and effects of altitude are making my handwriting almost illegible.

There is no easy fix. Conscious, slow breathing helps. I count my heart rate, balance inhalation and exhalation. Coca leaf tea is good and chewing coca leaves, in volume, with *llipht'a*, even better. To be effective, you have to chew coca several times a day, both a palliative and preventive remedy. Llipht'a is black caustic alkaline paste used in minute amounts that aids in extracting the active alkaloid compounds from the crude coca leaves. Made by cooking vegetable ash from quinoa or cocoa, too much can burn the sensitive lining of gums and lips, so great care is taken by the Q'ero when combining it with coca leaves.

To clear the head, they recommend inhaling vaporized isopropyl alcohol or agua florida, floral perfumed water. A puff or two of a strong organic cigarette is good too (not right after the alcohol— one would not want to catch on fire). We are well prepared with an abundant supply of coca leaves for ceremonial offerings, gifts, and for our use, as well as agua florida and mapacho cigarettes. But I wonder if there is enough to protect my brain? Brain damage at extreme altitude has been documented by magnetic resonance imaging.

The climbing now is not at all like walking, but the heavy lifting of one leg at a time, putting each foot down carefully, so as not to slip on loose stones and gravel. It's not so much the danger of cuts and bruises, but the debilitating effort of picking oneself up afterwards that necessitates purposefully paced steps.

Every so often, I crane my neck under the weight of my pack to see Ausangate coming closer and closer. It rises higher and higher, grows more immense each time I look. But, after a while, even raising my head is too tiresome. I settle into the climb, steady in the placement of my feet so not to slip, trying not to get too far behind Sebastian, who though somewhat ahead of me, is also showing signs of fatigue. We slow to an imperceptible pace.

Breathing slow and deep, I pull in what little air I can, pray to the Apu for strength, holding before exhaling and with every breath there comes a richness of energy. The Chinese call it *chi* (or *qi);* the Q'ero call it *kallpa.* As we come closer, the life force of the Apu lends me *hatunkallpa,* much energy, and I feel lighter, and do not need to rest as often. My rhythm in slow motion, weaving between boulders, coming closer and closer to Ausangate, turns into a deep meditation, a fine synchrony.

~

A momentary vision of a frozen oasis, the great shimmering mountain goes out of sight as we move through a narrow ravine. The glacial lake that births the stream comes upon us suddenly. The side we approach is full of rough boulders, though many have been smoothed by centuries under the glacier that left them behind as the ice receded. We go in and around them, sometimes climbing over them. Of course this retards our progress, but it's necessary. There is no easy way around them.

Sebastian is unyielding now and keeps an unrelenting pace so we can camp before dark. We come to a gravel bar, likely once under water and ice. At last we find a place flat enough to pitch our two tents and make camp. But first, I walk to the lakeshore, still and opaque, the color of green slate. A blue gray glacier is at the far end and the snows of Ausangate are reflected in the lake's mirror.

The tranquility of the water reminds me of the American Zen Master, John Daido Lorri,[19] when referring to the thirteenth century Japanese Zen Master, Dogen, who said that water does not depend on mind or body, does not arise from karma, and is neither self-reliant nor-reliant on others: "Water, being dependent on water, is liberated."

Like the Chinese comparing the Tao to water: a still and clear mind is free of thought-generated intention—even the intention to become enlightened. Water, exists according to its nature, has no intention or non-intention. It cannot be any thing other than water, or its transformation into ice and snow, steam and clouds. Like water, the mountain is not in a state of becoming. Water and mountain are pure beings, enlightened ones by grace of their essential nature.

Water is water; mountain is mountain.

I take coca leaves, and select a perfect k'intu, perform the phukuyr'tti, and pray: "Apu Ausangate, great earth mother, Pachamama, sun father spirit Inti, lake water mother Qochamama, I am here."

I carefully chew the leaves, acutely aware from the effects of the coca, I harmonize my body mind with the spirit of the mountain. Then, choose another k'intu, and placing the three leaves gently on the water, I listen.

I hear nothing; the only sound is deep silence.

The leaves float as one, turn around several times. Then like sails catching the wind they are drawn across the lake toward the mountain like three small boats.

I watch until they are out of sight.

This lake, this mountain, and these clouds offer a magnificence beyond my transient life. For this moment, this time, this place, I and the water, I and the mountain, I and the coca leaves are one and the same.

On the edge of being, on the shore of sacred ground, we shimmer.

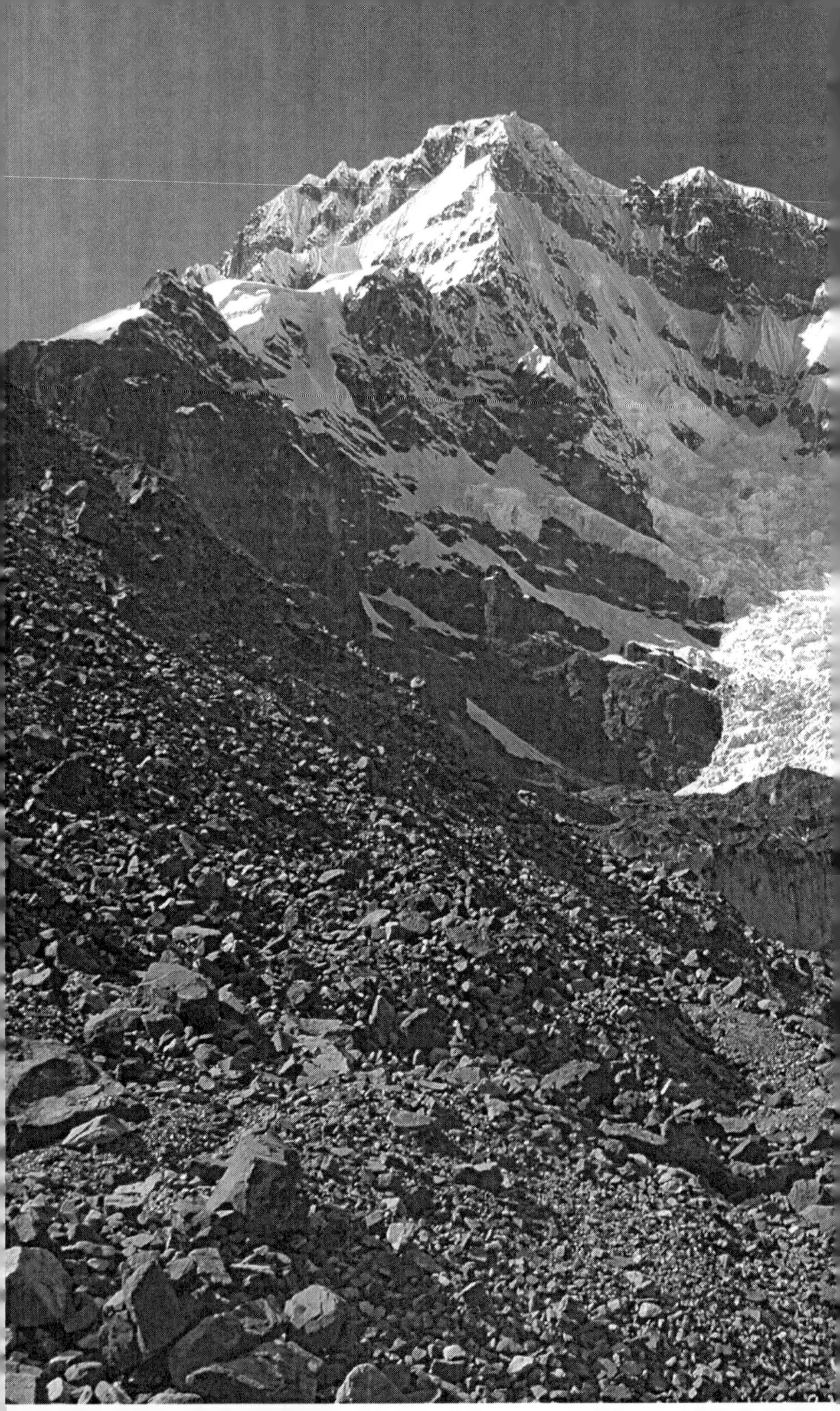

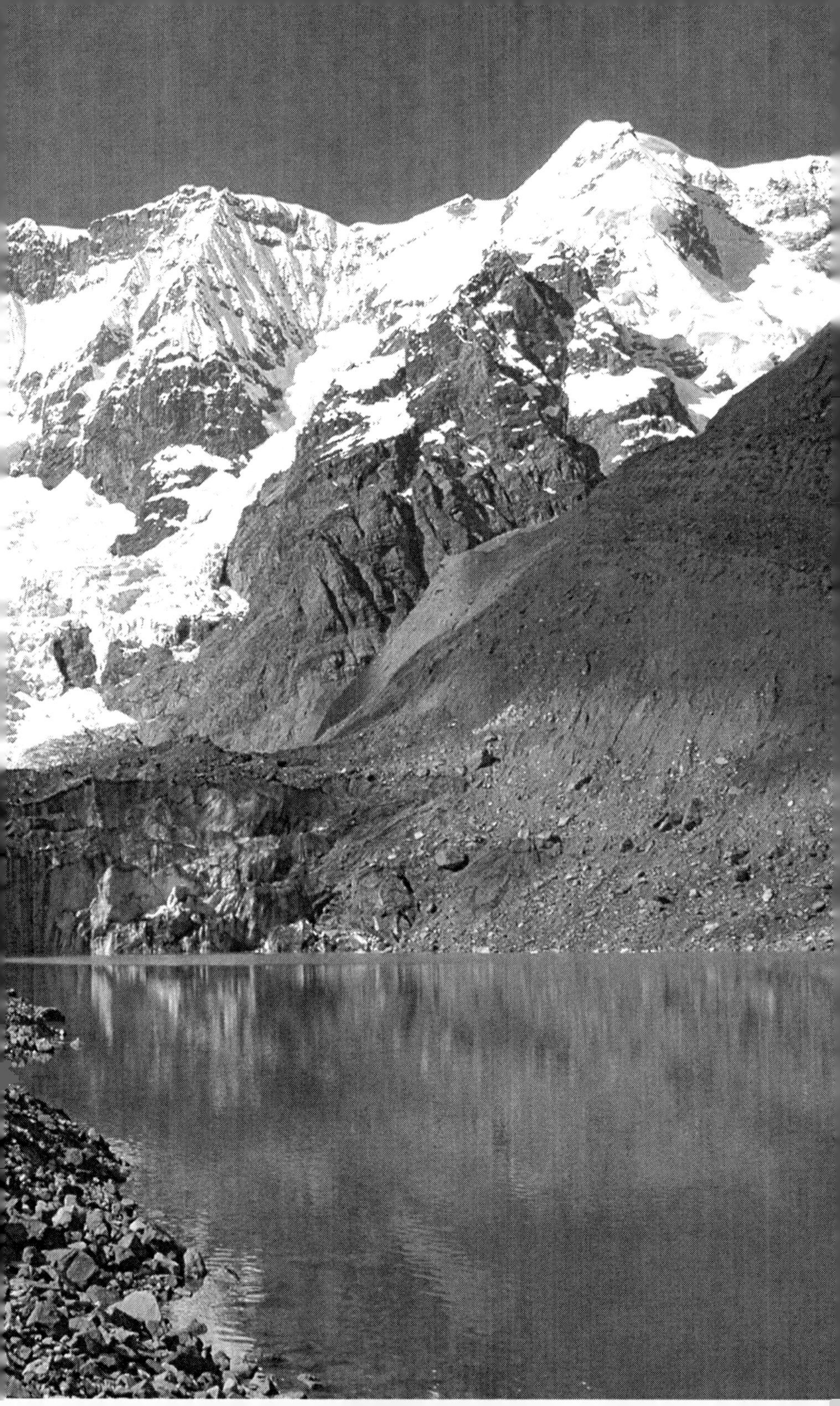

Previous page:

Glacier and lake at base of north face of Ausangate.

~ CHAPTER FIVE ~
# WHITE CLOUDS GREEN LAKE

This land where the Apus dwell is a sensate geography populated with spirits, laced with lines of energy linking invisible worlds; layered holographically, one nested amidst the other, living and interrelated, intimate with whispers between the unseen and the seen, the minute and the grand, the animate and inanimate, and between the Apu and the pakuq. To the initiated, the land and its creatures, and spirits communicate with the shaman. Highly sensitive to the movement of wind, the cry of birds, the flight of condor, shape and shadow of clouds, the color of stones, the shaman hears the baby bird cracking through the shell of the egg. He sees nature's infinite palate—nothing alike, nothing unalike. The variations of snow and sky, ice and stone are fraught with inescapable meaning that is nonetheless elusive.

To be receptive to the messages that are present—sometimes grand and meaningful, but mostly subtle and tenuous—he must be sensitive to small promptings, hidden messages, and whispers of wind, nuances of leaf. The shaman reads novels in the dance of insects and poetry in the dazzle of light on falling water. In such messages, he interprets the balance between human and animal, insect, plant, and mineral. Attuned to a higher order, harmonic and whole, the shaman can hear how the world began as told by a stone.[20]

Sometimes Pachamama speaks through lightning and thunder, sometimes through rainbows and sunsets. But mostly, there is silence when nothing needs telling, as if she has disappeared into the infinite—Pacha, time and space folded layer upon layer, universe upon universe, until the moment when ripples reappear on the thin envelope of biosphere, and the down on a condor's neck quivers as the first snow flake falls on the mountain.

Sebastian and I stand at the edge of an invisible bridge to the spirit world of the greatest Apu. Before us is a green lake, behind the lake the slate blue glacier, above the glacier lies the snowfield, and high on the rock face overhung by wind-sculpted snow resides the heart of Ausangate.

He sees patterns, flow and balance. To see this way, one has to embrace an approach based on waiting, quietude, alive to the present. Sebastian informs me that the most powerful Apus are characteristically still. The shaman imitates this stillness. Then, issuing from the profound silence of the heights comes every sound. Absolute stillness ushers in every spiritual molecule of nature. Pure white light is the manifestation of the spirit of the great Apu, he says. Clear, impersonal, clarifying light.

~

Our bare camp is within a crescent of outcroppings—dark rocks dusted in white with great fissures lodged full of compressed snow turning to gray ice containing aggregates of pebbles. The glacier is to the left and the snowfields of the massif rim it round. The pinnacle of Ausangate reaches skyward, stationary, immortal. In the twilight, the lake becomes the green color of jade. The moon, nearing full, crests the peaks to the east, and is reflected in that sheen of green.

When the sun drops behind the western ridge, the night will quickly turn frigid. There is little time to waste, and we work methodically and quickly clearing sharp rocks and stones in an area just large enough to pitch two tents. I am breathless and lightheaded with the work and I realize, too late, that it might have been better

Chapter Five: White Clouds Green Lake

to acclimatize more slowly. The mountaineering rule is not to ascend more than 1,000 feet per day. We started in Cuzco at 10,800 feet, drove to Tinki at 12,190 feet, and then walked to Pacchanta at 13,900. We pushed upward to our first camp at 14,500 feet when we should have slept at Tinki. In one day we went 3,700 feet higher. Today we climbed to over 19,000 feet, another 4,500 feet, a distance and change in altitude that should have taken us four days. The effort leaves me exhausted.

At 19,000 feet the air is arctic, and so thin it's almost nonexistent. Though I am well-adapted to high altitude after more than a decade of repeated climbs in the Andes, I find that above 14,000 feet it turns difficult; at 16,000 feet it's a struggle; at more than 18,000 feet, even the Q'ero find it challenging, and I find it on the edge of... impossible. I can imagine what it is like at 20,000 feet, but shudder when considering what it is like to push the impossible, to enter the "death zone" above 25,000 feet where time collapses, as those who summit Mt. Everest, called Chomolungma in Tibetan or Sagarmatha in Nepalese, meaning "holy mother," the mother of all Apus. But we are not here to conquer. We have come to listen and learn, to be still, and to do so we must only be close enough to hear.

My heart is racing to circulate more blood. I make an effort to slow down my breathing and calm my heart rate. I inhale deeply, lengthening my breath in an equal rhythm of inhalation and exhalation. For a moment, I am concerned: Will I get enough air?

How long will I be able to stay this high?

It's too late for second thoughts. The only solution is descent to a lower elevation, but that is not going to happen. We are here for several more days, and have brought provisions for eight days should the Apu require us to stay.

I am extremely thirsty, my lips are parched and cracked open from intense sun and dryness. My face, even with the application of strong sunscreen is red and swollen. Warm soup will prevent dehydration, but it is not filling. At this altitude, it takes longer to cook our soup of potatoes, and I am anxious to eat, my appetite having returned suddenly, but Sebastian is patient as he waits for the water to boil. Our dinner is simple: lake water and boiled potatoes, and a few thin slices of carrot and onion, with no salt.

We eat quietly, sharing the one pot of potato soup equally, downing first one bowl and then another, and finally dividing the remains between us. Warmed from the inside, we huddle down. The meal is minimal, and yet nourishing enough to sustain us in an environment where only short grasses and the hardiest of herbs survive. No insects live up here, no birds, nor lizards.

Minute-by-minute the cold approaches, real as ice forming on the lake, silent as a puma. I wear quilted long underwear, heavy muslin pants, two flannel shirts and a red down vest, and over that a down jacket, and on top of the jacket a traditional Q'ero poncho. On my head and covering my ears is the traditional Andean knitted cap. Despite this protection, the cold is penetrating, stiffening. I am chilled to the bone.

My mind slows to the pace of glacial ice. I cannot think clearly. Taking field notes is arduous. The best I can do is scribble using abbreviated words, sometimes sideways on the page, incomplete, broken. Thoughts give out. I am reduced to mists of mental blindness. My personality is thinner. It is not needed here. I do not miss it.

~

The dark between moonrise and sunset has settled in, and the first stars appear in a sky that in a few hours will be jeweled. The lake, ink black and all but gone, makes sibilant sounds as a faint wind rises above the rippling water. The glacier is alive. I feel it breathing in the night.

I am again reminded of words from Han Shan, who took his name from where he lived, *Cold Mountain:* [21]

> *In the mountains it's cold.*
> *Always been cold, not just this year.*
> *And here I am, high on mountains,*
> *Peering and peering, but I can't even see the sky.*
> *Moonlight on Cold Mountain is white.*
> *Silent knowledge—the spirit is enlightened of itself.* [22]

Chapter Five: White Clouds Green Lake

My reverie is fleeting. At this elevation, I am concerned more about sleeping than poetry. Although I am accustomed to the rigors of high altitude during the day when the sun is strong and the air is warm, nights can be tortuous. Lying prone makes it hard to breathe; my heart labors and my lungs fill with fluid. There is a heavy pressure in my chest. In the past, due to sleep apnea, I experienced startled waking, bolting up gasping for air—disorientation and freewheeling anxiety caused by weird dreams, my mind skidding on an icy slope of panic. I am haunted by my dream from Urubamba and the apparition in Cusco. Will they reappear up here in a nightmare? Will I wake to lose my mind entirely?

In this rarified of elements, some of it is already dream like, some remembered, Sebastian tells me that some of life is a dream, waking reality and dreaming scarcely distinguishable. The dream is not separate, he says. That's why we are here. Entering the zone of non-ordinary reality for me is transformational. For him, it is navigating the seamlessness of the universe, what he was born to.

But danger lies in missing steps, being impatient, pushing too hard in the wrong direction, and confused behavior can cause poor judgment, memory loss, and hallucinations. Even temporary disorientation can lead to loss of bearing, a dangerous condition when in remote wilderness where there is no rescue. Even some Q'ero have been known to wander aimlessly in the mountains and disappear without a trace.

∼

Sebastian has put on a red wool sweater over his traditional black alpaca under garments, and over that his finest ceremonial red poncho. He spreads his common daily wear poncho on the ground, sets a multicolored uncuño in the center, and pours out a large mound of coca leaves.

"Pichukuka," he calls me to join him, oblivious of the falling temperature.

It is time to drive away the effects of high altitude, center ourselves and unite our spirits to single-mindedly harness our purpose on the mountain with our destiny.

A phosphorescent halo of moonlight shines crescent above the eastern crags in the clear night sky. The lake, mirroring the moon, provides enough light to see by. Ausangate, draped in snow, is illuminated in the darkness.

Sebastian carefully selects k'intus, one leaf at a time, placing each set of three leaves between his fingers until one hand is full of three trios of coca, nine leaves in all. I follow his example selecting k'intus of my own. He passes one to me in the formal way: hands symmetrical, thumb and first two fingers gently clasping the three leaves.

Accepting the first k'intu in front of Ausangate, I dedicate myself to the work. I stand up, face the lake and mountain, and perform the phukuyr'tti, blowing breath, my life force into the leaves, humbly asking the Apu permission to approach, to honor our efforts. I do not petition for the Apu's presence, knowing it will come if the time is right. Traditionally, it is Sebastian's role to invoke the Apu, not mine. I am simply hoping for a good ceremony in the company of a true man who loves Pachamama with all his heart.

We choose more leaves and pass k'intus to each other, praying with each cluster, chewing methodically for the better part of an hour, now and then adding tiny sticky black pieces of llipht'a to maximize the action of the coca. Within a few minutes, I experience the distinctive intense anesthetic effect in my cheeks and tongue, following by a lifting of fatigue, clarity of mind, and mild euphoria. With thick wads of masticated coca leaves tucked between upper teeth and gums, temporarily, the temperature feels warmer and we can talk without the distraction of shivering.

Sebastian begins: "We are here for one purpose," his voice taking up the space of night. "But, first," he asks, respectfully, "I must know your intention. Speak from your heart, Santiago. Tell the Apu why you are here."

"Apu Ausangate, I commit to this journey, this path of Ayni, and will walk it to the best of my ability until the end of my life. Sebastian, you will always be in my heart even when I am far away. I cannot be here all of the time and my home is distant, much farther from here than to the coast of Lima, but I will return again and again. If I am to die here, do not take my body back. Present it to the Apu and let the condors consume my remains."

"*Allin!*" he exclaims. "Excellent!"

Our hearts are wide open. Sebastian nods, giving me his tacit approval that this moment was destined to be; that all is right with the world. In the moonlight, there is a glint of white teeth, a brief smile. Then Sebastian's face is again impenetrable, his expression a reflection of what is around us—moon, mountain, lake, emptiness.

"You have lived the way of the Q'ero in your own skin. Now, you are one of us. Do your best. Think clearly. Set your goal. Never waver. If the Apu accepts you, Ausangate will be at your back."

We chew more coca leaves; then he begins again: "Keep a clear heart and a strong mind. Guide others by your example and from your experience, and you will stay ahead."

He reminds me that the true man leads by his presence, not by his words. It is the meaning you make from your life and that you provide to others that is important. The Q'ero, like other traditional indigenous people I've known, hold actions higher than words, but also value heart-felt speech that indicates a commitment of purpose, an honesty of intent, and humbleness in the face of Pachamama. I know we are the same in our desire to create a sustainable future and teach others the way of Ayni, yet we are different in incomprehensible ways. We share core values, but our social and cultural worlds are far apart. His is rooted in ancient traditions; mine is rootless, sometimes, and generations removed from Sebastian's innate reverence for nature. It has taken the better part of my adult life to become reacquainted with Pachamama consciousness. It has taken decades for me to overcome acculturated prejudices, to go beyond "ego-driven spirituality," and to keep my body fit for the physical rigors of the shaman's path.

Sebastian continues: "This is the time when you step into the void; into the arms of Pachamama. You are already awki, compadre Santiago. You are pakuq, shaman. One day you will become Apu."

I am stunned by his announcement. Those who dedicate their

lives to understanding the laws of nature and following the path of Ayni with integrity, may, upon their death, permeate a shrine or unusually shaped natural place with their energy. As in Europe in centuries past when saints blessed a grotto or spring or forest, or in India and China where temples are created over the meditation place where a yogi or Buddhist monk achieved enlightenment, spiritual energy presides in such places and sanctity remains for years, even centuries. The Q'ero build no temples, the mountains are sacred enough. When energy becomes itself, limitations no longer apply, and a man can become the mountain, or the mountain a man.

"Tomorrow we start cleansing. Before the main despacho takes place we will purify ourselves by water with quartz and white flowers where the stream leaves the lake. This is the site of rushing water where purification is best. After the cleansing ritual, I will offer five despachos: one for each of the minor Apus, a personal despacho for you, and a principle ceremony for Apu Ausangate. We stay up all night for the main ceremony and wait for the Apu."

"You will endure the Orcopuntakarpay. It will make or break you. There are four possibilities. If you are well prepared and the Apu accepts you, then you become altomisayoq, the supreme shaman. The Apu will always be at your service and will bestow the power of seven spirits to assist you. However, even with such power you will be limited to these seven spirits. By working exclusively with them you can accomplish a lot but it drains your energy and your life is short. You are here, now the Apu must choose you."

"How will I know if the Apu picks me?"

"That is easy," he says. "The Apu will try to kill you."

In the Andes, being struck by lightening is a sure sign that one is chosen by the Apus. Other signs involve coming face to face with a puma, or getting lost but surviving long periods alone in the wilderness.

"The second possibility is that the spirits come, but they do not remain. You have to return and try again. You will have to come back three times, maybe more. The third possibility is that the spirits do not come at all and you will go no further on the path of shamanic power."

"And the fourth?" I ask.

"The fourth possibility is that nothing tangible happens right away. No spirits come and the mountain does not speak, but after two or three months, your life begins to bloom in spontaneous and inexplicable ways. Balance enters."

"Does this balance bring peace?"

Sebastian pauses, and then continues, "The garden of your heart flourishes and blooms. The results may not come right away. It could take months or longer to happen. This is the rarest of all four possibilities."

"The Orcopuntakarpay is your choice," he says seriously. "We can do other ceremonies and leave this one if you are not ready, but if you decide that this is your time, it will close the doors to all lesser Apus and open the door to the highest energy, Apu Ausangate. You must choose a way to use the Apu's energy that will come to you. It must be something to work on over a long period of time. When you are accepted, the Apu will always be there for you, backing you up, guiding your work and efforts."

Sebastian always speaks clearly, without doubt, as if every thing is predetermined. I reach for more definition.

"And this work, is it different from daily life or a profession?"

"It is spiritual work and the results are apparent when living the way of Ayni. But, it could take the form of a direction in your career, or maybe something entirely new."

Though he used the Spanish word, *"trabajo,"* I know he does not mean the drudgery that is associated with doing a job you dislike. If your work grinds you down, something is out of balance; you are not in Pachamama's flow. The outcome of spiritual work is not a product, though it might also include producing things or results, but the creation of a state of being that is good, meaningful, lasting, and true. It is the quality within that is significant and living deep values make it sustainable.

In his mind, there is nothing greater. Embodying the essence of Pachamama in one's heart over a lifetime, every aspect of daily life is the spiritual work of Ayni.

It is bitterly cold. I struggle to listen, wrap my poncho tighter around me. A raw wind hisses over the ice. The moon is anchored in the sky above the lake. Clouds form to the east spilling over the far peaks like great white rivers.

"*Chiri chiri,*" Sebastian says. "It's very chilly. It's been a hard long walk to this camp. You did well, compadre. My heart is content and I said what I wanted to say and you listened well. Our bodies need rest. Let's sleep."

I am exhausted, and sleep comes easily, but I wake every few hours gasping for air so that I have to sit up and consciously slow-breathe. My head pounds and feels heavy, as if twice its weight. In the hopes of relieving the pressure and pain, if due to dehydration, I sip on a powdered electrolyte mix, but it doesn't help much. For the rest of the night, my sleep is sporadic, but by morning, I feel better. The headache is less and over the next several days it will become tolerable. However, it doesn't go away altogether until we return to lower elevation at Tinki.

~

I wake to the whistle of the propane stove. Sebastian is up. I notice his movements, spare and smooth, are slower than at lower elevations. But other than slow motion, he seems all but immune to the effects I'm experiencing.

The first order of the day is potato soup. I join him and we wash and prepare potatoes for the pot. The high carbohydrate diet is the ideal fuel for walking, the fluid and minerals in the broth prevent dehydration. However, the low fat content does not provide enough thermogenic support to keep warm. We consume the potato soup to the last drop of thick starchy broth, and tidy up bowls and spoons, cover the stove. We will eat one more meal in the afternoon; the same basic fare of boiled potatoes with a few chopped vegetables, but it will not be until we have completed the ceremonies that a spoon of coarse salt is added.

The sky is blue and brilliant, the lake covered in ice. Not a thin glaze, but frozen thick enough during the night so that it will take

Chapter Five: White Clouds Green Lake

the rest of the day to melt and even then there will be large sheets afloat on the water. Booming sounds come from the mountain as massive chunks of ice sheer off the glacier and crash into the water. Avalanches cascade off vertical mountain walls, the clouds of white powder absent of sound the way thunder follows lightning. Several seconds later, there comes a tremendous explosion, the distance between us and the pinnacle being several kilometers, slamming us with violent intensity, a reminder of the power of this place.

Snow upon snow. Light upon light. Blue upon blue.

It is time for the morning lesson, and Sebastian lays out an uncuño. He pours out coca leaves and examines them in great detail.

"Compadre, did you dream last night?" He asks.

"No. I did not dream last night."

I am thankful that the headache is almost gone, but am exhausted from broken sleep. Sebastian slept well, but he says it was very cold, and his sleep was not as deep as usual. He says he had a short dream about a hummingbird that turned into a low-flying hawk, then into a condor.

The dream tells of a powerful but small spirit that transforms three times. First it appears as a hummingbird, *q'ente,* the messenger between this world, kaypacha, and the upper one, hananpacha, and carries medicine and healing formulas that it writes with its beak. The hawk, *anka,* is a warrior, swift and fierce, defiant and unrelenting, and yet patient. The third transformation is the condor, *kuntur,* which flies higher than all creatures, higher than an Apu, and represents hananpacha. This final transformation takes the spirit in the dream to the Apu and then beyond the peak, as it flies into the higher atmosphere close to pure spirit.

Letting the meaning of the dream live, complete in the telling, we exchange k'intus and chew coca in silence. What is beyond peak experience? When you have gone as far and as high as possible, what lies beyond the condor's wings, where becoming transforms into being?

The sun is rising higher, but it's still behind the mountain, and as it comes closer to cresting Ausangate, golden rays form a star burst over the pinnacle.

"Munaycha!" Sebastian exclaims. "We are surrounded by beauty." With the recognition of nature's innate beauty, munay, he begins the day's lesson: "Before birth, only munay exists."

According to the Q'ero worldview, love and beauty are inseparably intertwined, ever present in nature, and inherent in the human soul, the primary state of consciousness, the state of being where we come from and that which we return to. Therefore, munaycha means, all is beautiful around me, and infers that I am in love with the world. Our true state is pure being manifested as love and beauty. But we are spiritually asleep unaware that munay is all there is.

"Our earthly journey starts in our mother's womb, bathed in munay. When we are born our consciousness is connected to munay. The simple consciousness of little children is still great in munay. But little by little, we drift away from our spiritual source. We find the world a harsh and frightening place, so return to our mother's breast where it is warm and safe. Learning to stand up and walk is difficult. We fall down. It hurts. We are nourished by breast milk, and the safety of the breast is comforting, so we come crying back to her when we totter and stumble. Little by little, we learn. First, instinctively with the loving guidance of our mother; later from our father, who teaches sternly. Our grandparents and elders are all love and wisdom. They provide security, the sense that if we study well, we can also be wise. Learning is yachay. We learn about planting and harvesting, caring for the alpacas, and the correct manner for ceremonies. We learn by imitation of our father, then from stories, and later by instruction on rituals and about the Apus from wise elders and our pakuqs. Then we apply what we learn. We make mistakes but keep trying until we get it right. This is llank'ay. Right action. Over a lifetime, as we mature, learning begets knowledge, and then wisdom comes."

Sebastian explains the three cornerstone principles of the Andean way: munay, yachay, llank'ay—to feel, to think, and to be. Munay is love and beauty. Yachay is learning, knowledge, and wisdom. And, llank'ay is right action and meaningful work. Together they form a trio, like a coca k'intu; like the three levels of existence: ukhupacha, kaypacha, hananpacha.

Our earthly journey begins, and if we live a good life, will end in munay. At first, munay is a gift of the great mother, Pachamama, and from the little mother, the woman in whose womb we were nurtured. But later it must be earned. We come into the world embraced by munay, and if our life is whole and balanced, if we practice Ayni with a good heart, we can be born again into the consciousness called *munaykawsay*—the way of being in love and beauty.

"Some want greater fulfillment in life, to serve others, or are called by the Apus to be more; so follow the way of the pakuq. Some go higher; learn from a sage, the *Willaq Uma,* the fully integrated human and master spiritual teacher. You can also learn directly from spirit through mystical experiences with the plant teachers, *ayahuasca* and *huachuma.* Dreams can also teach. Compadre, you have known all of these. But, the most powerful calling is when lightning strikes the ground near you, or when it strikes you. *Hillap'a* comes from hananpacha and is the servant of the Apus. Those called to the shaman's path learn through sacrifice, like you and I have done, and the physical and mental suffering of being in the high mountains, in caves, or the deep forest alone. The pakuq is called and trained to help others, to tend to their suffering, to calm their fears, to heal, to translate dreams, and speak to spirits."

Weird creaking sounds echo off the mountains as the glacier shifts and the snow pack on the north face of Ausangate awakens. Sebastian turns toward the mountain, pauses, continues.

"But, our deepest longing is to return to paradise. The original state of consciousness, munay."

He describes the state of munay as the bliss beyond comprehension, the beauty that transcends words. I draw comparison from Eastern philosophy: Is it like what in India is called *ananda?* The Dalai Lama explains that those who arrive at spiritual bliss are in the same state as the Buddha, *sugata,* in Sanskrit, the one who has reached bliss. Is it possible that in the New World, the great ancient civilizations like the Inkas had a spiritual tradition parallel to the East? Is the deeper meaning of munay comparable to the bliss of Buddha nature? Is there a universal spiritual philosophy that is cross-cultural, timeless, and transcends human religions and belief systems?

As we live out our life, Ayni is what holds everything together, keeps things in their rightful place, promotes healthy society, protects those that cannot care for themselves, and assures that our children will have the same opportunities as we have.

"Today, I help you. Tomorrow, you help me." He pauses giving space to his words, and then adds. "This is every day Ayni. Without it, community doesn't hold together. As we grow up, little by little we get further and further away from munay. If we follow Ayni, there is balance. We can return to munay. But, if we forget the way home, if we neglect to practice Ayni in our daily life and ignore the cycles of nature, things fall apart. Pachamama is forgotten. We lose balance. We are no longer embraced in munay."

"Hai," I respond softly. "The further we are from munay, the more unhappy we become."

Sebastian nods in approval, softly chewing coca leaves.

"Go on," he encourages, "you're talking well."

"Ayni is the spiritual path of Pachamama."

Is the way of Ayni an answer to our modern angst, the solution to Sebastian's dilemma?

"This is our responsibility, compadre," he says completing my thought. "We shall bring Ayni to others, not just Andean people. Maybe there is still time to save Pachamama. Perhaps we can find a way home, back to munay. This is what Apu Ausangate may teach us."

He is finished. The rest of the morning we prepare ourselves for the noon cleansing ceremony. Sebastian begins to wash and sort small white flowers we bought in the market in Cusco, and arranges them in small bundles. I take notes and photograph the lake, but even in the warming sun, the air is cold and the effects of altitude tiring.

∼

Chapter Five: White Clouds Green Lake

The sun is midway between sunrise and sunset. May is fall in the Andes, and because soon it will be the winter solstice, the sun is not directly overhead, but traverses a southern path that passes just above the peak of Ausangate and descends in an arc to the right of the mountain. Sebastian has been following the sun's trajectory and testing the temperature of the water all morning. He finds a place where the glacial lake pours down into a rushing stream, tumbling over room-sized boulders, heading north into the Urubamba River, that merges in the Ucayali River; then turn east into the Amazon. All rivers from the Peruvian Andes eventually run east; all join the mighty Amazon.

The lake is immaculate. He chooses a place of clear knee deep water just before it tumbles into the stream. The shore is layered with gray stones, but some are green like jade, and mixed in are pieces of white flint, some palm sized. With the warming sun, the ice has receded towards the glacier, though large sheets float about, some close to the shore. A cerulean sky, clear of clouds, forms the midday canopy. There is no wind, though for a moment, faint ripples appear on the water, running across the lake as if chased by unseen forces.

Sebastian and I gather small pieces of quartz washed ashore down steam where he says they have been purified by the torrent. He pounds them into a coarse powder; stone upon stone, in a natural basin formed by the stream.

We strip down to the waist, he in black alpaca leggings and I in khaki muslin pants. Barefoot and bare-chested, we sit on a tabletop rock near the shore to share coca leaves. The sun is warm now, but the air remains chilly. I form a k'intu and carry it to the water's edge. Praying to the spirit of the lake, I gently place it on the surface of the water. At first the leaves drift towards the glacier, but then pulled by the current generated by the force of the steam, they are drawn toward the headwater until the coca leaves plunge downward swallowed by the power of water.

Sebastian stands, hold his k'intu toward heaven, and prays to Apu Ausangate: "Come spirit mountain, come energy of sky and water, snow and ice. Bring medicine for the people. Hanpuy. Hanpuy."

He places his leaves on the water and they drift upon the lake untouched by the current, slowly move along the shore, then the wind pushes them towards the mountain. We make many more k'intus, letting them float where they will, some plunging downward in the stream, but many move across the lake like small rafts set adrift. On some we have put white flower petals and these shine in the sunlight.

Squatting by the shore, we chew coca leaves until the spirit of uramama is strong within us. I feel lighter, warmer, and my breathing comes easier. The lake is like polished green marble. The mountains and snow, and the glacier are reflected photographically perfect. Our k'intus have disappeared over the water.

As the sun arrives at its apex to the right of Ausangate peak, Sebastian stands, and facing the lake, says, "It is time to clean away the past. Be strong."

I touch the water gently with my fingertips, like a blind man reading braille, feeling for the soul of the lake, interpreting the message of water. There is no bird sound, no wind, and Sebastian moves by me silent as a cat. I dip out a handful of water with my hands, as clear as diamond and ice cold, and sprinkle drops on my *misaq'epe,* the traditional Q'ero ceremonial bundle of alpaca wool, red with diamond shaped black lines, designs representing Inti, the sun.

The Q'ero take ceremonial preparations very seriously. Signs and permission from the Apus comes first. Then the cleansing process begins with water, flowers and herbs, then with stones, followed with smoke, and finally by fire. First, we must be washed clean physically and mentally. We remove our pants and naked, present ourselves to the lake. Sebastian gathers the ground quartz in an uncuño and steps into the lake with water up to his ankles, wades in to his knees, and beckons me to follow.

Trembling, I step into the glacial water. It is unbelievably frigid, but convincing myself that I can stand it, wade in close to Sebastian who uses his hands to pour water over my body. It is freezing, and my ankles and legs begin to ache severely—like my bones are being cracked open. The water is far colder than I anticipated, and the aching rapidly becomes more intense, and I quake uncontrollably. Within minutes my leg muscles cramp painfully and my body tightens. The air chills and the water is unbearable, numbing, but I will myself not to splash back to shore.

In front of me, further out in the shallow water along the shore is a flat rock large enough to stand on, and I make for it. Sebastian follows, as if to protect me, and as I stand up on the rock, he remains in the water, and scours my skin with crushed quartz, chanting an ancient song of purification in sacred runasimi, pours more icy water over me and follows with a sprinkling of crushed white flowers, smelling of jasmine. I stand on the rock, naked in the glacial lake, blue sky above, white mountains to all sides, a pale yellow sun to my back equidistant from dawn to night, and spread my arms wide, turn palms to Apu, open my heart.

Sebastian walks into the lake until he is thigh deep; and treating it like bathwater, immerses himself, holding his breath under the water, standing up slowly, shaking his head, his black hair sending drops of water in all directions, casting staccato notes upon the lake, which dance and sparkle with light.

"*Sumaqchay!*" he shouts. "It's great!"

He makes for the shore, where he rubs himself with quartz and covers his head and body with white petals. I follow slowly, my bones aching, stepping gingerly along the stony bottom. When on shore, I use one of our cooking pots to pour water over him to wash off pieces of stone and flower.

The first stage of the cleansing ritual complete, we hold sacred space with the lake. I clench teeth against the residing chill that seems to have entered my blood, stiffening me from the inside, but he is relaxed and in good spirits. I use my poncho to dry myself, for we have not brought towels or soap. Everything we do is in the old way as much as possible, minimal. We stand on the shore in the sun for what little warmth it offers. The noon sunshine is fleeting and the air already has an edge; in the shadow of clouds, I quake from the cold.

When mostly dry, I quickly dress and wrap myself in my poncho. Sebastian dries off in the air, and dresses himself piece by piece, as if reluctant to wear clothes at all.

Though Sebastian has detailed preparations to complete for the all night vigil, he suggests we rest first. It is going to be a long night, but for this moment, we sit together in a wedge of sunlight, a boulder warm against our backs, watching the water go viridian, green stone and blue sky merge as the sun moves lower in the heavens.

There is no trace that we have been in the lake. Its surface is serene.

Tired from days of walking, the warm sun makes us sleepy. Sebastian curls on his poncho, but cannot sleep. The coming ritual must be on his mind. I am exhausted and retire to my tent, but before falling into a deep afternoon sleep, I attempt to write field notes, capturing fragments of the cleansing ritual, lonely scratches on a white page. Lines of rugged poetry written in soft calligraphy are made at lower elevations. The slow crossing, range after range, distance upon distance garner grains of truth by which black ink comes alive. Here, ink freezes. I only have blank pages.

In the heights of Ausangate, my inner and outer selves come apart.

Consciousness expands. Mind ceases to exist.

There is only mountain and emptiness.

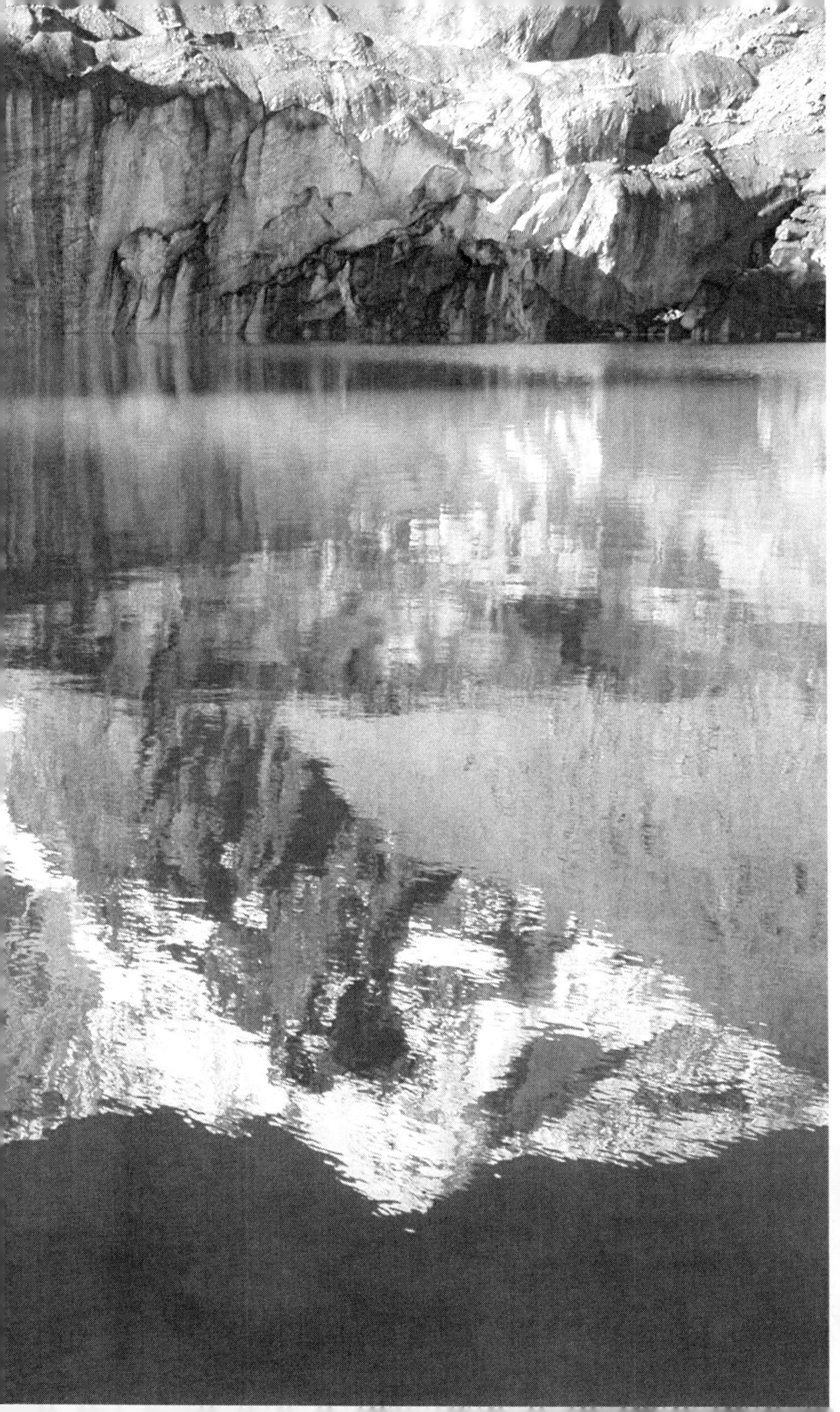

Previous page:

Reflections of glacial ice.

Chapter Six

BLUE TRANSPARENT

Clouds, thick during the night, wispy white lines in the morning, have vanished and the sky is transparent. The higher we've gone, the thinner the veil of sky until now, close to the top of the world, the air is so light, it's almost nonexistent, but the dome of heaven is more intense and under it, I can hardly breathe. In the shadow of the mountain, memory is intangible. Most of my experiences escape; the process of forgetting is already begun. Whatever I am is being erased by the wind, lost in clouds and snow. Where lies the perfect empty mirror? Where falls the condor feather? How silent is the snow and ice? How thin is the blue canopy of sky?

Sebastian is already at work. He has chosen a place for the ceremony near the shoreline facing Ausangate. Three large stones serve as backrests and windbreak. He meticulously clears the area in front of the stone backrests for us to sit without being jabbed by rough-edged pebbles. There he folds a wool blanket on top of which he spreads his everyday beige poncho. Now he levels the ground directly in front where we will do our misa work, conduct despachos, rituals of respect and reciprocity.

He brought with him a bundle of thin green branches that he ties into small crosses and others into circles, to which he attaches fragrant white flowers with cotton thread. Sebastian offers their perfume to the mountain by waving them in the air, while whispering prayers in the old tongue. I help Sebastian make more than a dozen, the exact number is a secret, he informs me, and places them in the shallow water at the edge of the lake to keep the flowers from wilting.

"These are offerings to the awkikuna. The spirits will come in the night to find out who you are and what we are doing here. It's good to be prepared."

Natural places like springs, grottos and caves, or the great trees in the rainforest, have special powers and harbor nature spirits called awkikuna *(-kuna* at the end of a word forms the plural in Quechua). According to the Q'ero, every plant embodies its own unique spirit that is a repository of that plant family's knowledge, including ways to use it for healing. Sacred teaching plants like Ayahuasca have very powerful spirits and serve as guides into the spiritual dimensions and the realm of the dead. The awkikuna can also dwell in lakes, especially those that form around an Apu, acting as protectors of the place, servants of an Apu; or tricksters, or worse, malicious spirits intent on harming. It is for this reason that Sebastian prepares dream catchers adored with white flowers.

The first level of Q'ero knowledge is encoded in Ayni. This is when you learn about Ayni. The second level, aynikawsay, when you live Ayni, involves mastery of the awkikuna. Then these tricky entities are enlisted as allies, guides to the world of primal memory, the personal and collective subconscious. The more powerful ones can grant healing ability, facilitate precognition, and serve as guides in the spirit world. Though they can lie dormant for ages, wrathful ones often guard the portal to the realm of the Apu. There they can block entry, obstruct passage through the mountains, or create storms. They can manipulate the subconscious and instill irrational fears, causing doubt and dread. This is the realm of the underworld, the subconscious mind, ukhupacha, and when underworld fears cross into normal reality, paranoia, delusions, and delirium can occur.

Sebastian informs me that it is important to be clear-headed, to root out doubts, to master fear. Then the awkikuna will welcome the shaman, facilitate the process as servants to the aspirant. Only a pakuq of single-minded intention can approach an Apu.

"What do the offerings mean," I ask.

"The white flowers tell that we are here to talk with the Apu. The circle is the symbol of Pachamama and the cross represents the four directions."

White is the color of the Apus. The four directions, *quatro suyus* in Spanish, and Tahuantinsuyu in Quechua, is the name for the Kingdom of the Four Realms, the Inkan Empire. In the Q'ero cosmovision, the world is created from a mutual pair of opposite forces, which divides once into another pair—one makes two, and two begets four—to form the four cardinal directions of the world. Cusco, the Inkan capital, is at the axis of the four directions, the "navel of the world."

These small gifts of cross and circle covered in white flower petals and sweet perfume serve as offerings to the awkikuna of the lake, informing them that we come with a good heart to speak with the Apu. They also help to create sacred space, screening out and protecting us from malevolent spirits, preventing them from entering our ceremonial circle.

"Tonight some of these offerings will be in front of us, and one cross will be on each side, and to the front and back. When we enter the circle, you cannot leave for any reason. This is the first rule of the ceremony."

"Are there other rules?" I ask.

"Yes, there are many rules, but this one is the most important. It is the framework of our intention, the most important aspect of the shaman's path. This is the lair of the Apu. To withstand the presence of the Apu, you have to be unmovable, indestructible."

By indestructible, he means you have to stand firm, fearful perhaps, but with an unwavering purpose. Within, your intention must be one pointed, purified by many years of shamanic practice and personal sacrifice, and therefore indestructible. But firm does not mean inflexible, because if you are too rigid, you break. In shamanic undertakings, pushing the body and mind to their limits is essential, but dangerous. Should fragmentation occur, the soul can escape through cracks in your psyche, and will eject, as if under pressure, if the cracks become fissures, separating soul from body in a dramatic and bewildering manner.

"There are powers in this place that do not like to be disturbed and can cause you irreparable harm. Once, I worked with a Q'ero man who attempted a ceremony requiring unwavering intention, but he became impatient and stepped beyond his circle and nearly died. Other pakuqs could not help him, so I was called. When I saw him, he had been unconscious for almost a week. I told his family that his soul was gone far away and there was little I could do. They begged me to try. After many days of ceremonies and offerings to the Apukuna, awkikuna, and Pachamama that I buried in the earth in the old way, he woke up. We were all thankful for his return. Now he is normal, but timid, and will not go near places of power."

Sebastian completes three larger crosses, to which he attaches many more white flowers. "These are presents for the Apu, should it appear."

He bends some branches into large circles and attaches white petals with thread forming a crude web to serve as dream catchers. I place them between the lake and us, inhibiting malicious energy from disturbing our ceremony. He directs me to put the crosses, braced with rocks so they won't blow over, at four corners around us. The stone, protecting our back and sides, is at the center of the sacred circle.

There is an order to where we sit, the same one that we always take in ceremonies: I am to his left, and when family or other Q'ero shamans are present, they sit to his right. When there is just the two of us, I still sit to his left, and on his right are offerings of wine and *aqha*, chicha in common Quechua. A fermented beverage made by sprouting and then fermenting kernels of corn, aqha is produced by soaking the kernels in water for several days until soft; then a starter is added providing a culture of friendly bacteria and enzymes necessary for fermentation. The finished product is a sticky white gruel that is slightly sour with an alcohol content of about one percent, just high enough to cause dizziness. Besides offerings of aqha, we also have pure cane alcohol, Peruvian red wine, and a bottle of cheap champagne, and a large number of coca leaves. Sebastian organizes each offering to his right within easy grasp. In addition, I have brought a bottle of Pisco, the Peruvian distilled liquor made from grapes that I macerated with coca leaves, and place to my left, next to my coca leaf bag.

We have several bottles of agua florida, floral scented water useful for purifying the ceremonial space and for cleansing sacred stones, *misarumi*. Its fragrant smell lightens the energy, uplifts the spirit, and just as a beekeeper uses smoke to calm angry bees, the scented water pacifies the awkikuna. In Q'ero shamanism, energy is considered to be light or heavy. Light energy is uplifting and healing, heavy energy weights down and causes obstruction and disease. Agua florida keeps the energy light.

~

The afternoon deepens, the sun moves as if in time lapse across the mountaintops. The lake becomes reflective, silver in the shallows and dark, almost black, in the deeper water close to the glacier. The glacier itself is smoky blue, gray streaked. Above it and beyond the snowfield, clouds form fast from water vapor rising up from the humid jungles to the east—thick walls of white hugging the rock face, folding over the edges of stone, blending into the whiteness of snow.

Sebastian places red and black *mantas,* a woman's shawl, also called *llikla,* to the front of where we will sit. He places his *mamaq'epe,* the sacred bundle, wrapped in a dedicated llikla, to the center front. He arranges red and white carnations; the petals will go into the despachos, the two colors signify *yanantin,* mutual opposites—male and female, left and right—white for the snow covered Apus, red for the blood of Pachamama.

We brought red kantutas, the sacred flower of the Andes, favored by hummingbirds and the awkikuna. To the Q'ero, hummingbirds, of which Peru has the most species in the world, are considered among the four sacred animals: condor, puma, serpent, and hummingbird. In Quechua q'ente, in Spanish *colibri*, hummingbirds are thought to travel between this world, kaypacha, and the higher spiritual realms, hananpacha, carrying messages from the Apus. They can seek souls lost in ukhupacha. They also serve the spirit of the master plant teacher, Ayahuasca, carrying healing messages to the shaman, writing the prescription with their beak. The kantutas will not go into the ritual offering. They represent the hummingbird and are used solely to pacify the awkikuna.

Sebastian sits back to evaluate his work and then closes his eyes composing the ceremony in his mind. I look to the mountain, then to the lake. It changes color from dark blue to light green. Clouds build and recede, reappear between crags and around snowdrifts. High above is a small black spec in the sky. Riding thermals, never once moving a wing, a condor soars near the white pinnacle of Ausangate.

"Kuntur," he says, as if having sensed it and points with his eyes skyward.

The Andean condor[23] is the largest raptor of the world, and with a wingspan of over ten feet it can reach soaring heights of 23,000 feet, higher than Ausangate. They are long lived with a lifespan of about seventy years. For these reasons, condors are revered in the Andes as the bird of the Apus, the representative of hananpacha, the one that flies the highest, the bird of souls, taking the spirits of animals and humans to the afterlife.

The puma engenders yanantin, bringing balance to this world, kaypacha. The serpent, amaru, rules the lower world, ukhupacha, where it consumes and transforms negative energy into lighter, cleaner, spiritual energy. And, the hummingbird is the messenger between them all.

Sebastian takes the sighting near the peak as a good omen. The condor sighting informs him that the Apu is listening, Pachamama is participating, messengers are flying overhead, and we have permission to proceed. Now that his preparations are complete, mine are just beginning.

"It is time to cleanse your misa. Prepare it for the Apu. Wash each stone with love and charge each crystal with your best intention. Rinse them in the rushing water of the stream. When your misa is dry, keep it close to your body; do not open it again until tonight. Make coca leaves into twelve k'intus for the despacho. Everything has to be right."

"I understand, *papito*," I reply. "I will do everything with care and love."

After following the stream down from where it pours from the lake, I find a spot with a protected bank made of finely tumbled stones where a deep pool forms in front of several large boulders that face downstream. Brushing the flashing water with my fingertips, I pray to the local awkikuna, the spirits of this place, and to the water, the spirit of life, and offer three coca leaves, letting them pour over the rapids. I place three more on a flat stone, holding them in place with a piece of quartz I found in the stream, offering them to water and sky.

My misa contains the sacred stones Sebastian gave me years before, and are carried in a dedicated hand-woven pouch with red and black lines, designs symbolizing *Hatun Inti,* the Great Spirit behind the Sun. A dark vertical line woven down the center, separates left and right halves of the design: reverse images paired together, the right side representing the morning sun and the left the afternoon sun; the line dividing the two is symbolic of midday when the sun is suspended overhead between morning and afternoon.

I have another pouch for carrying coca leaves, a *kukawyaka*, bigger and of the same color scheme, but with larger and bolder designs in the center, representing *Ch'unchu,* the symbol for Inkari wearing a feathered headdress—the return of the Inka. I gently touch each *wyaka,* familiar with the feel, tightly woven and warm to the touch. In this lunar-like gray and beige landscape, these pouches are reminders of the colors of life: red is blood, green for plants, yellow is the sun, and black is the fertile earth.

I empty a small amount of coca leaves on an uncuño, shaking out remaining pieces of leaves from the kukawyaka, being sure to get them all. I turn the pouch inside out, open my misa, and spread out another uncuño with red and black alpaca threads. Then carefully wash my shamanic tools, each stone and crystal, in the icy water three times. Holding each one skyward for the sun to recharge them, and offering more coca leaves to the mountain spirits, I pray: "Apu Ausangate, grandfather, give life to these stones. Accept this offering of coca. I dedicate them to your service."

Then, placing each stone and crystal on a clean uncuño, I go inward. Entering a deep meditation, where there is only here and now, this mountain. I am in a place where time falls away.

The sun is warm now, my headache is gone, and the Andean air dries the thick alpaca cloth within minutes. By comparison, a night in Lima might be one hundred percent humidity, and it can take a week for an alpaca cloth to dry. The cleansing and dedication of my misa complete, I return to camp. Sebastian has begun boiling water for our meal of potato soup.

"When the night comes, the moon will rise here," he indicates this with a slight lift of his chin. "Just before it crests the rim of Ausangate. Eat now. Rest. It will be a long cold night. I will call you for the ceremony."

Inti, the Sun moves northwest in the direction of Machu Picchu, the winter arc, the ecliptic path of the Sun across the sky, abbreviated, its warmth weakened. On the equator the Sun is not directly overhead in the winter, which happens only two days a year, once on each of the equinoxes. Within minutes it is frigid. We eat quickly, and to avoid the cold, I retreat into my tent to write and rest.

Later, wind ruffles the tent flap. I cannot sleep. Anticipation of the ceremony keeps me alert. I sit and face the mountain to meditate, which comes effortlessly, perhaps due to my light-headedness. But my meditation is abbreviated by troublesome thoughts. I am concerned about the responsibility all this requires. I know that there is no guarantee that giving all will admit me to the realm of the Apus. I can only hold to this place, this Apu, these people.

Soon, the wind stops. Stillness returns. Like waves settle when

Chapter One: Sebastian's Dilemma

the wind ceases, my anxiety leaves on its own. With my misa at my side, I fall asleep.

~

The weather has changed again, unpredictable as ever. Clear for several days, it's turned windy and heavy gray clouds have now hidden the mountain and glacier. Has the Apu closed the door on us?

Sebastian is concerned about the weather. It will be a long night, and conditions around the mountain change fast. Should it turn bad, we will not complete the ceremony and it could get very hard for us. Just in case, should things go wrong, he stores our gear and braces it with heavy stones. For now, he suggests more rest, and we lie down together to wait.

I stir awake and Sebastian notices. The wind is quieter, but the mountain remains hidden in dense clouds. The preparations for the ceremony that open the Orcopuntakarpay are complete. It is time, and we begin even though the mountain is concealed.

He sits cross-legged and I do the same, sitting to his left. We put our misas up front on specially prepared mantas—ceremonial textiles called *q'epenallepas*—but we do not open them. For now, it is important to keep our shamanic stones concealed. A *kukauncuño* goes directly in front and dedicated *misauncuños* are placed to the right and left, ready for sacred stones and ceremonial offerings.

Sebastian takes an enormous bag of coca leaves from his q'epe and randomly choosing a handful, selects twelve leaves for divination. For the Q'ero and other Quechua, potatoes, llamas, alpaca, and coca form a seamless interrelationship with Pachamama, the Apus, and humans. Reading meaning into coca leaves is a way of asserting the connection between Apu and pakuq, the one whose ally resides in the place no person can venture, the highest of the perpetually snow-covered peaks—the Apus.

Before we go further, he needs to read the will of Ausangate. With repeated wrist flicks, he snaps coca leaves down on the uncuño, interpreting what he sees. If the leaves line up, we may proceed.

The leaves fall and patterns emerge. Leaves that are whole and complete, signify prosperity. One long leaf, says there in one man, Santiago, in the midst of wholeness, the uniformly shaped leaves. Then, a double-formed leaf appears, one stem producing dual ribs, the two leaves joined as one, signifying good fortune. And then one, brilliant green leaf, the last to fall, lands on top of the pile of coca leaves. This is what Sebastian is looking for. The spiritual impact of our presence on the mountain is now assured. The leaves have lined up. We can proceed with the ceremony.

We begin to sort k'intus, first collecting misshaped leaves and putting them aside for offerings to the awkikuna of ukhupacha. Then the most perfectly shaped leaves, arranging them in trios according to size and shape. I help and place them in stacks of nine, three k'intus per group.

"Prepare your despacho, compadre," he instructs me.

A wind has picked up and blows coca leaves into the lake. I palm the twelve k'intus I prepared earlier and arrange them on the upper edge of my uncuño, using small stones to keep them in place. I make a personal despacho and he prepares three: one to call the Apu, and another to present should the Apu appear, and the third one as an offering for the glacier and lake tomorrow.

Despachos are ceremonial offerings, symbolic acts of Ayni made in appreciation for Pachamama and the Apus. They range from simple to elaborate. For karpays, initiations and distinctive events, the complete Andean cosmovision is recreated in fabric and plants, flowers and ribbons, seeds and sweets, and the soft inner fur of llama and alpaca. For major karpays, a dried llama fetus is decorated in gold and silver. In Inkan times, real precious metals were used. Now, foil and beads serve as symbolic substitutes.

This ceremony demands bare, simple ritual, so my misa is in the old way using natural colored alpaca uncuños. I make my despacho in the traditional manner starting with a k'intu in the center of a plain uncuño, adding white alpaca fat, untu; then more coca leaves that are covered in white carnation petals and quartz. It is simple, and under the moonlight, elegant.

Sebastian's two despachos are also small ones, but more colorful and contain sweets and seeds, downy condor feathers, and many more coca leaves. The one for the lake has red and black *huayruru* seeds[24] favored offerings to the awkikuna that dwell in the underworld of ukhupacha.

The moon is near full circle radiance, and already rising higher in the east, behind Ausangate. Clouds obscure it from view; but it is bright enough to illuminate the clouds that glow like a gigantic paper lantern. The night deepens and we wait for midnight.

After more than an hour of silence, watching the lake darken and the moon rise to our left, Sebastian takes out a reed flute and plays simple, haunting notes, staccato and repetitive.

The wind stills to quiet. As I watch, the clouds thin to nothing. The full moon appears over the pinnacle; silver against black sky, so bright it drowns the stars in radiance. Flute sounds fill the spaces between lake and mountain, between stones and snow.

Another hour passes. It's getting considerably colder. Sebastian looks at me, and smiles, his teeth gleam in the moonlight: "The Apu awaits," he says.

Sebastian prepares for the hatun despacho, the primary ceremonial offering for the Orcopuntakarpay. He takes his mamaq'epe, "mother sacred bundle," the dedicated ceremonial bundle storing his shamanic tools, unwraps it carefully, organizing his objects including several small wooden cups called *qeros* (pronounced "kero," like Q'ero, but unrelated in meaning), and a white alpaca fur bag, *phuquchu,* made from a new born alpaca that died a natural death ritually symbolic of offering itself to the Apukuna, and which he fills with coca leaves.

He forms a kukak'intu, faces the mountain, and calls in a strong voice, "Apu Ausangate, I offer this k'intu and ask you to bless our work and receive our offerings."

Then he passes the kukak'intu to me, and I stand, face the mountain and perform the phukuyr'tti and pray: "Pachamama, great cosmic mother. Apu Ausangate, great grandfather mountain, protect and bless our work, open the way for greater service for the good of the people, and all things."

Sebastian pours wine and aqha into the wooden cups and seashells, and sprinkles some on to the ground remembering Pachamama, and flicks more into the air for the Apu. I do the same with Pisco, aspirating a small amount into my mouth, mixing it with my breath and forcibly blowing it out, aerosolized into the air...illuminated by moonlight.

Sebastian opens his misaq'epe and takes a colorful sheet of gift wrap paper, folds it into half and then half again symbolizing the four directions, and lays it out open on an uncuño. In the center he places vicuna inner fur, and on top the misshapen coca leaves as offerings to the awkikuna residents of ukhupacha.

Taking the first k'intu, I hand it to him in a ritual manner using both hands, the three leaves clasped between the first three fingers of each hand. He blows on the k'intu and begins to build from the center of the paper outward. Creating the despacho layer upon layer, he ritually adds ceremonial offerings of corn, coca seeds, spices and herbs, alpaca fat, gold and silver foil, more coca leaves, and a llama fetus covered in colored beads. When the offering is close to completion, he requests the kuka k'intus that I made earlier, he asks me to blow into them seven times, while I make my silent, heartfelt request to Apu Ausangate. Then he places them with extraordinary care along the upper border of the offering.

Sebastian presents me with a black stone. It's large and heavy, dark and smooth. I receive it open-palmed, sprinkle it with agua florida, and hold it heavenward, thanking the Apu for our blessing tonight and acknowledging Sebastian for his friendship and teaching and place it carefully on my own misaq'epe.

When finished, he folds the paper over the offering, wraps it in the uncuño, and folds the mamaq'epe around it all, and taking the entire bundle, we stand up and he brushes it over my body, blows on to the top of my skull, and passes it to me to blow into nine times. This is done for healing, for harmonizing soul with body, mind with heart, reconnecting the individual with Pachamama, energizing the entire being to receive the Apu.

Earlier, while it was still light enough to see, he prepared a ceremonial fire with dry grass and alpaca dung he gathered along our route to the mountain. We have also brought a small bundle of dry wood and when I pour agua florida on the pyre and touch it with a match, it bursts aflame.

We kneel in front of the fire, facing lake and mountain. Warmth, at last! He presses his lips to the bundle, his words muffled by the cloth, and from the deepest part of his being, invokes the Apu to bless our quest. Then, he opens the bundle and taking the offering wrapped in blue paper, lovingly places it on the fire. Instantaneously, it blazes and sparks flash and fly, burning through the edges and then bursting aflame as the alpaca fat fuels the fire.

"*Sumaq!*" He exclaims. "Wonderful."

We watch as the flames consume the offering. This is purification by fire. Then he pours aqha and wine to the earth, and I offer Pisco to the lake pouring drops onto the water, a prayer offered with each ring upon the water; and flick more into the air for the pleasure of the Apu.

The fire burns bright and warm, but soon fades to embers. We wait until the last glow sinks to dark ashes. With the fire out, I shake in the bone-chilling air. Even my tongue is chilled. Clouds materialize over the glacier forming a halo around the base of the mountain; the peak visible reaching up touching the platinum moon that shimmers above, but I am too tired to hold onto the beauty of the moment. The implication of the ceremony loses its hold. The lake turns to ice. My ritually cleansed body quakes in the night.

I am at the intersection of my life, where the ancient overlaps the modern, the "once was" presses on the "soon-to-be."

At this moment there is nothing but the mountain and the moon.

We sit through the darkness, long into the night.

There is no wind. Everything is still.

All is silent. Everything waits upon transformation.

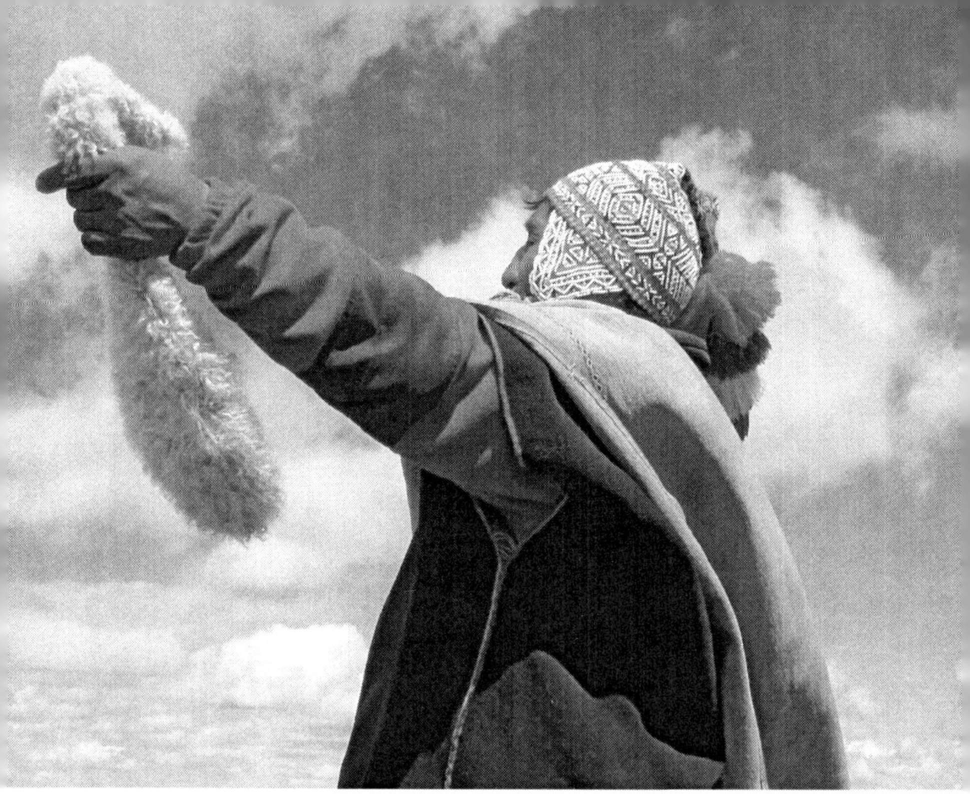

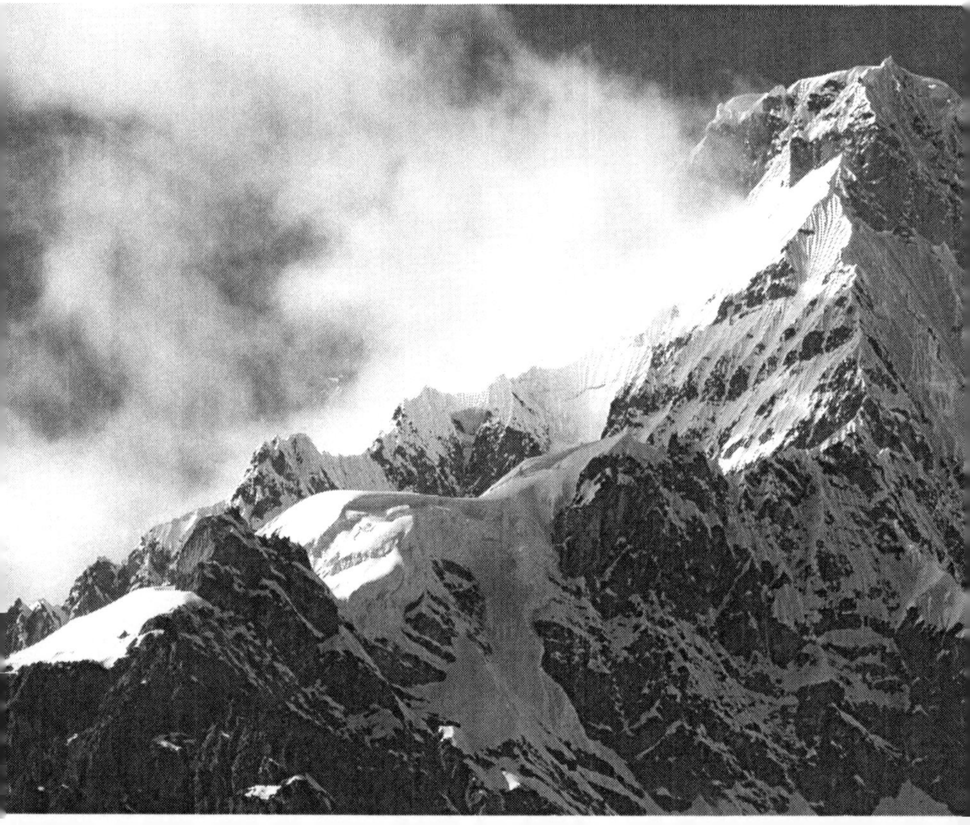

Previous page:

Above: Sebastian calling the Apu.

Below: Ausangate peak, northeast approach.

~ CHAPTER SEVEN ~
# THE LAST MOUNTAIN

The morning sky is gray with dense clouds. New ice, formed during the night, lies thick on the lake and rims the shore with crystals. In the midday sun, they will turn to liquid. During the night, the snowpack on the mountain walls settled. With the full moon, the temperature dropped enough to halt avalanches, but eerie creaking sounds come from the glacier as if immense furniture were being rearranged. As the day warms, falling snow masses the size of houses will likely begin again. For now, all is frozen into stillness.

Sebastian is up already, boiling water. He motions me to drink mate de coca. There will be no meal until evening. Coca leaves will sustain us today.

We sit together facing Ausangate. The sun is still behind the mountain. As yet no shadows reach across the lake.

"Find a place along the edge of the lake. Take your misa. Watch for Inti to crest the mountain. Wait for the Apu." Sebastian tells me how to prepare for the next step in the initiation, not giving orders but simply stating what to do.

"What do I wait for?" I ask.

For a Taoist, waiting is not passive, but a form of patient ferocity like the puma before it springs. For the Q'ero, waiting means enduring. This kind of waiting requires implicit trust in Pachamama and a steeled confidence that you will know when the time is right to act.

We sip on the dark mate, coca leaves packed tightly in the tin cups, requiring me to move them aside with a finger tip, the bitterness not unpleasant, the heat warming and welcome. Sebastian takes some wet leaves up with his fingers and chews them. Our eyes meet.

"Here, the Apu is the teacher," he says. "You are prepared. You will learn."

"What then?" I wonder aloud.

"Compadre, when there is no time, no questions and no answers, then the Apu is present."

Sebastian wants me to honor the possibility of my dream, to complete our quest, and to take the journey that I was meant to make. I cannot empty myself, Zen-like, of all thoughts, desires, and worries. I am more like the cup of tea half full, adding water and drinking, pouring in more without additional tea leaves, until the cup is full of pure, clear water. I cannot patiently wait over a lifetime, like the Taoist, for the wind to stir on the lake of consciousness. But like falling snow, when there is no other way, I can surrender to Pachamama.

I understand that my expectations of myself, perhaps even of this place, are too high and maybe a little romantic, or unrealistic. But I do accept that the Apu is a palpable enigma, and so will wait as he directs me.

We drink our mate in silence. The mountain is quiet. This morning, there is no booming as the snow mass shifts; no crashing of ice blocks as they sheer from the glacier. There is only the sound of two men drinking tea and chewing coca leaves. We pour hot tea drops on the stones as an offering to Pachamama, and steam rises up and is instantly consumed in the crisp air. In front of the mountain, we offer each other k'intus, whispering to the Apu. Can you hear me Ausangate?

I may not be ready to respond to the Apu's koan, but I can give my heart and pray: "Thank you, Pachamama, for this time and place, for our breath of life, for these clouds, for this beauty that surrounds me. I am here."

"Remembering is also Ayni." Sebastian speaks into the silence.

"But now, let it all go. Your courage, endurance, and intention were required last night. Today, your heart will lead the way. The Apu knows what is in our hearts. When there is nothing to hide, the Apu will come. Prepare yourself."

Taking my misa and kukawayaka, coca leaf pouch, I find a place of smooth stones softened by centuries of water and chiseled round by ice. I sit cross-legged facing the mountain, the frozen lake dark greenish gray in front, and close my eyes. Meditation comes easily here.

After about thirty minutes, I soften my eyes, letting them open slowly. The clouds have thinned and clear sky appears. The round moon remains faint in a sapphire sky, the rising sun hidden behind Ausangate. Then, it crests the mountain and the snow turns molten gold fringed with pink. Fingers of shadow reach across the glacier. As the sun crests a knife-edged ridge to the left of the peak, sunlight streams onto the snowfield, covers the glacier in light, reaches across the lake, and rises up the mountain walls. Along the lakeshore, ice crystals glisten and crackle as the air warms.

I am lifted into the morning light. Taking three k'intus, I blow on the nine perfectly shaped leaves, fanning them against my lips, mingling breath and air. Performing the phukuyr'tti, I offer myself to the Apu: "Apu Ausangate, I am here. I offer this kukak'intu in your name. Great one. Ausangate. I have come. I am here, waiting."

My thoughts loosen their grip. My mind goes empty. My heart opens and my eyes close on their own.

Stillness, existence, pure being—mountain aware of itself.

～

After several minutes, I sense a presence and open my eyes to thin slits of awareness. A light, brighter than the sun, appears below the Ausangate pinnacle on the upper north face of the mountain. At first, I think it is sunlight refracted on snow, but it is stationary. The yellow sun, now well above the peak, transforms the world to the daytime colors of the Andes; shades of gray, iron blue, jade green, and opalescent white. I sense a gentle tension in the landscape. Pachamama holds her breath.

As I sit, a ray of white light emanates from the heart of the mountain, radiates over the snowfield and glacier, and across the lake to the center of my chest. I am breathless. There is no sensation other than the visual presence of the ray of pure light. It does not glow or emanate heat; I am neither transported, nor transfixed, simply seated, touched by the light.

After a few minutes, I feel radiant integration, effulgence around my heart and across my chest. Then the light gradually becomes transparent as air, and is gone.

I walk to the place of our night vigil, where Sebastian is waiting, divining with coca leaves. Six k'intus line the upper part of his uncuño, and several odd shaped leaves are arranged in groups on the left and right edges. He sifts through a pile of leaves looking for messages from the Apu, takes up several of the coca leaves he put to the side, and holding up a fan-shaped leaf, speaks: "This one tells us that we will complete the karpay and the day will be good."

He holds up another that is unusually long and thin, "This one represents the direct way to the Apu. It is powerful sign."

The sun is warmer, melting the ice edge along the shore. The shaded places are still ice bound and snow covered. In the shadow of the mountain, large stones sit round and white like eggs.

We sit together chewing coca leaves, and as the cocaine sharpens my mind, words come to me: "Papa, there was a disc of white light from up there." I point to the place. "It came straight, without a bend or change in diameter to the center of my chest."

"Did you feel anything," he asks, holding the straight long leaf.

"No definite sensation, neither heat or cold. It was neutral and pleasant, and I was not afraid."

"The Apu has engraved your heart," he whispers.

"What does it mean?"

"Santiago, it does not mean anything. Pure light is the essence of

Chapter Five: The Last Mountain

the great Apus. When they appear, they come as white light."

"Was our ceremony last night successful? Are we complete?"

"Yes. The Apu has responded, but it's not the end, only the beginning." He is whispering, never once taking his eyes off the mountain. "For the Apu to reveal itself is a great thing."

～

The day is upon us, but I am exhausted from the all-night vigil, and suffer from a spell of altitude sickness with intermittent nausea and episodes of tachycardia, and though the massive headache of the first few days has subsided, the entire right side of my face is swollen from fluid accumulation. I worry about the same happening to my brain, lungs, and heart. I will not be able to stay here much longer. Sebastian prepares me for the final step of the initiation. He is insistent that all signs including what the coca leaves reveal must be parallel and congruent before the next step can occur.

"The way is clear. We will go higher, Santiago, as close as we can onto the great Apu. It is dangerous. I do not want you to take any chances. Be careful. The signs are favorable. We go now."

Because Apus are sacred to the Q'ero, sanctuaries above the lives of humans, absent of plants and animals, void of every distraction of lower elevations, the ground is holy and not meant to be walked upon, mountain peaks not meant to be summited. We go close only when summoned by the Apu. Once at the base of the mountain, we can only proceed when granted permission by the spirits of the place. Sebastian believes we prepared well, made generous offerings, and the signs are favorable in the coca leaves. If the glacier and snowpack do not turn us back today, we will go higher, and closer. He places his misa and phuquchu, along with more coca leaves, into his carrying bundle and slinging it over his shoulder, cries out,

"Haku."

The sun is coming strong. It feels warm enough to leave my down parka at camp. I slip on my cap and shoulder my misa and kukawayaka, and follow along after Sebastian.

We proceed along the east side of the lake, working our way over a wedge of loose gravel towards the glacier. In the previous days, avalanches had fallen only on the right side. Though the terrain of the left side is more difficult, Sebastian deems it safer.

The closer we get, the larger the rocks become until they are a field of rough boulders. Some are the size of trucks that we must jump across one to the other. Deep caverns gape between them. My early morning mystical experience is gone, and now I am engaged in a kind of calculated athleticism. Such mental mathematics pits awkikuna magic against my monkish spirit. Silent endurance is the way, but one slip and the journey ends. I hesitate, thinking it over, but Sebastian urges me on.

"Compadre, you are thinking too much."

We help each other, arms locked at times; pulling ourselves over the last of what was once a massive landslide. Past the giant boulders, the slope is steep; we go tediously slow. Ponderous. Diagonally upward. Specs on the mountain. Breathing labored. I am lightheaded.

Across the lake, the ice has receded. I look up. To the north, Apu Sinakara is aglow, golden. In 2004, we performed ceremonies high on this sacred Apu. I am elated to see it, and the sighting lends roundness to my time in the Andes. Renewed, I go on.

Sebastian finds a way to move up and on to the far side of the glacier, but we have to cross a sixty-degree sloop of loose gravel and black dirt exposed from a recent landslide. He goes first, one step at a time, testing each foothold firmly before lifting the next foot, marking a trail for me to follow. I step across, placing my feet in each of his footsteps. It feels solid, yet pebbles spill and roll down towards the lake and splash into the water far below, giving me the impression that all of it could collapse and we'd plunge into the frigid lake.

When we are across and on firmer footing, he indicates that we can go higher still but cautions me from walking over the glacier. There are hidden crevasses and we have no rope for rescue. Instead, we'll skirt the edge. The going is not only difficult because of the rocks and ice, but we have gone several hundred feet higher. I can

Chapter Five: The Last Mountain

hardly breathe. I keep on, but have to rest, and breathe deeply every ten steps. I soon grow concerned about our progress. Will we make it back before nightfall?

Using his bundle, Sebastian passes an end to me and pulls me up and over the last of several boulders jammed together. We stand at the border of the snowfield. To our front is a blazing white expanse. Vertically above, is the north face—black rock, etched with snow and ice. The presence of the mountain is awesome.

We continue to work our way up until the mountain wall stops us. Pausing on a flat area, we prepare our misas and coca leaves for an offering. In front of us, wreathed in fiery snow, is the white wall of Ausangate.

Sebastian lifts his creamy white phuquchu, the pakuq's alpaca fetus bag filled with coca leaves used to call the Apus, holds it over head towards the mountain and in a loud voice performs the *haiwariquy*, the ritual summoning of the Apu in sacred Runasimi:

> *"Anchakaypampa, Pachamama.*
> *Jinallatac anchakaypampac, Apun.*
> *Jinallatac noccac juccarec, Apuy.*
> *Conancca sumaclla."*

As Sebastian prays, my heart opens. Eyes wide, I look to the summit; thin filaments of cloud come close. Blue sky appears in patches, sunlight breaks through the wisps of clouds and sparkles on the snow.

Sebastian has warned me that jealous ears are everywhere, even among the invisible forces of nature, and thus, not to arouse the awkikuna, we talk little and I keep my thoughts to a minimum, trusting my heart.

"From here, you go alone," he instructs as he finishes his prayer. "Take your misa and kukawayaka. Find a good place. Pray from your heart. Make your offering of coca to the Apu. Return here when you are finished. Go slowly. The snow is firm, but it can slide under you."

"Hai," I acknowledge his warning and veiling my concern I agree to pay attention. But, the truth is, I am worried. The snow has been coming apart for days, dropping off the cliff face, collapsing in great sheets, and exploding into the air. Even footsteps planted with care are dangerous under such conditions, the weight of snow perilous.

"Do not be afraid. Go. I wait here for you."

～

I find the snow granular and firm with a few inches of powder on top. It is not slippery; still I test each step, and head for a rock outcropping about a hundred feet across the snowfield. Above and to my left, clouds coalesce in front on my eyes. First blue sky and sunlight, now delicate threads of cloud. I look upon a lunarscape of tepid sun through dappled clouds.

I move forward deliberately, incrementally slow. Sebastian is a small figure below. In the far distance, white peaks push above high plateaus through fields of clouds. In front of me, vapors materialize and multiply out of thin air, twisting into sheets of white cotton. I keep going, but the clouds thicken so that I quickly lose sight of the mountain peak and cannot see the glacier and lake below. In minutes I'm engulfed in white. The distinction between up and down, front from back disintegrates. All is opaque.

I remember when I lived with the Yupik Eskimo of St. Lawrence Island in the Bering Sea. In 1968, I survived several "white outs." Old memories return. Instinct takes over. Better to be closer to the ground. I kneel in the snow to wait it out.

With the clouds blocking the sun and without my parka, I shiver as much from anticipation as from cold, it's not freezing at midday. Lightheaded, I fumble with my misaq'epe, but gain control and holding it to my heart, begin to pray: "Apu Ausangate, I am here. I have followed my dream and have come to listen. Pachamama, I am here, on your sacred mountain."

I repeat this simple invocation, more a statement than a prayer, over and over, until it becomes a mantra. In the utter quiet, even a whisper, even a thought is too much noise; even a prayer is too loud. I become silent.

I am surrounded by stillness. Embraced by snow and clouds, I see nothing. All is white.

~

A figure approaches, as opaque as the clouds. At first I think it is Sebastian. As he comes closer, however, I see that it is not Sebastian. This man wears a poncho the creamy color of natural alpaca with thin red and blue lines woven into the edges. His ch'ulhu is the same neutral color with red tassels. The man stands twenty paces from me, oscillating in and out of focus, as if blending into the clouds.

Then words come as if they were all around and within me, as if the trillions of cells in my body had a voice.

> "These are transformational times. It is the end of an era, a grand cycle is closing, another not yet beginning."

I am aware of a rich softness that envelops me in a cocoon of snow and clouds, filled up by the resonant voice.

> "The spirit of the last mountain, Apu Ausangate, has retreated deep into the earth. It will go deeper still and then enter into a great slumber. This will last a very long time. When the world is ready, Ausangate will return."
>
> "Pachamama is at work changing her attire. Pachamama designs the course of things and knows all events. A set of instructions from the womb of the Great Mother is prepared as a guide. But, the fate of humanity is no longer predetermined. It is time for a revolution in the soul of humanity."
>
> "The world is on the threshold of its greatest challenge. This is a contest for the heart of every

> human being. Heroes will rise up and villains will attempt to defeat the purpose of good."

His tone is smooth, his voice clear, each word perfectly enunciated, without a hint of judgment, and without the least hesitation as if what he says is certain beyond belief.

I am neither here nor there, simply kneeling, cocooned in clouds and snow. It is as if I am in a dream; as if he is not there at all; as if he is painted into the clouds; merging from nothingness; as if the secret of the Andes has been apparent all the time.

> "Many have looked for the secret of the Andes in the wrong places. The secret is Ayni. It comes from the heart of the Great Mother, and lives in the pure heart. It is the essence of Pachamama."

I've seen the man before. My mind, stressed by my weakened physical state is slow to recognize the speaker who has come to me in the clouds. But now I know who he is—Suryamana.

Clouds, thick as wool a few moments ago, thin to lace now, slow dancing patches of gauze reveal glimpses of Ausangate peak with a backdrop of iridescent blue sky. As the vapors thin, the vision of Suryamana comes and goes: part sun, part clouds, part snow. Then blue sky breaks through, and Ausangate rises up, an immense wall of ice, snow, and stone.

From below, I see Sebastian coming steadily towards me, lifting one foot after the other, advancing in slow motion, placing each foot down carefully, silent as if walking on cotton, his mind clear and as steady as his steps. He moves in stillness. A contradiction that is Sebastian.

Lost in a timeless blur, I try to stir, but I cannot move my legs. My feet are numb. I want to make an offering, but fumble with my misa, and coca leaves fly out and my sacred stones tumble down in the snow.

Sebastian is here with me, putting his arms under mine from

behind, and he helps me to my feet.

"I am alright," I say, coming around.

He makes sure that I can stand on my own before letting go, and then looks around the snow in front of me, careful where he walks so as not to disturb any signs. He says there was a cloud that covered me completely; only until it cleared did he see me kneeling, motionless.

"There," he says pointing in front of me.

Are they puma prints? Larger than the size of my palm, one directly in front of the other, no shadows in the tracks because the sun is directly overhead, white-upon-white is a trail leading across the snowfield toward the east rim of the mountain. I doubt what I see because it is too high for even these resolute large mountain cats. Before I can get a closer look, a ground wind picks up, filling the tracks smooth.

"An Apu was here," Sebastian states as fact, standing motionless, having no need to examine them.

The mountain peak is to our front, the glacier and the lake far far below. We stand together in the snow, side by side, face the mountain, perform the phukuy'iti and offer coca k'intus, praying quietly, then holding silence, keeping sacred space as long as possible, eyes and hearts open, the sun moving over our shoulders.

I stand on hard-packed snow, white powder to my ankles, blowing up my legs. Sebastian is resolute, expressionless. Coca leaves drift around us over the snow. The sun, overhead now, is hot enough to burn skin but the atmosphere so thin and dry nothing melts, nothing changes.

My stones are gone. I've used the last of the coca leaves. My misaq'epe is empty.

In the realm of ebbing clouds, poetic snow, and cathedral mountains, the Taoist principle rings true: mountain is mountain.

In this place of retina-burning sunlight, breathlessness is all there is.

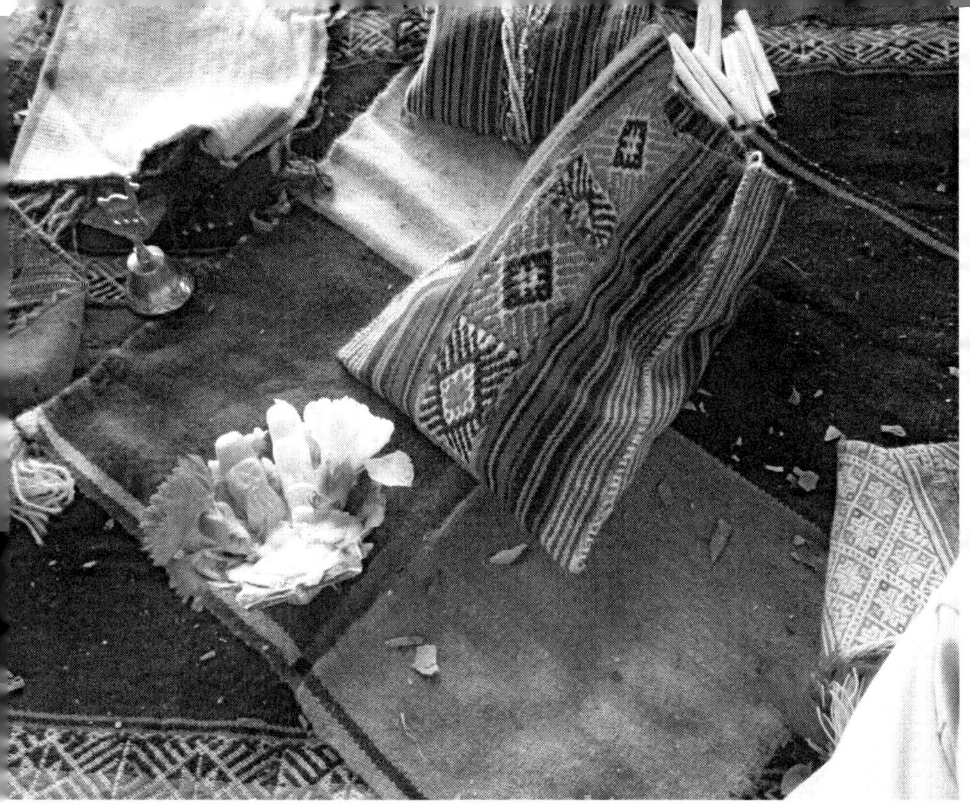

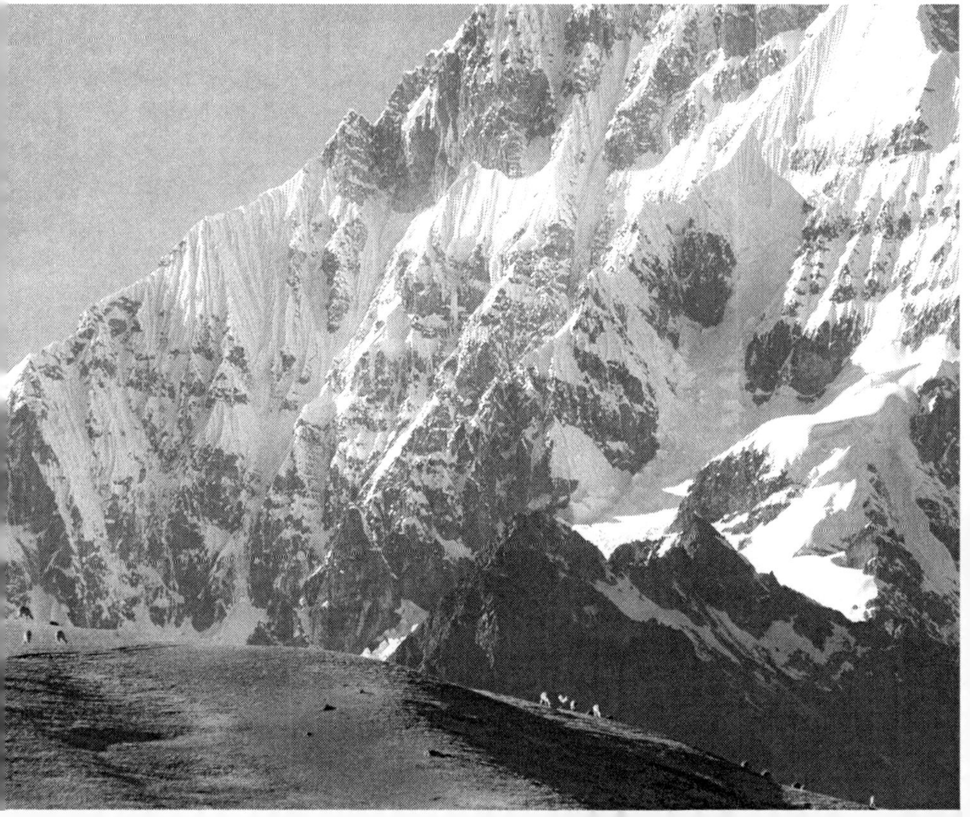

Previous page:

Above: Traditional Q'ero ceremonial cloths that form the misa.

Below: East wall of Ausangate.

EPILOGUE

October 2011

Since our journey to Ausangate, two events have further clarified the message of Apu Suryamana. The first was when I learned the glacier at the base of Ausangate was gone. Sebastian and Nicolas have returned several times to the mountain since our first visit in 2008. They told me that the entire glacier sheared from the mountain's rock face, broke completely apart, and slid into the lake. Over the intervening time, the great ice blocks melted and smaller ones were carried down river during the high water months of the rainy season. The gray blue glacier is no more.

The second event was meeting one of the last altomisayoqs of Q'ero. An altomisayoq is an oracle. To the Q'ero, oracles are portals through which the Apus speak directly to others. They provide wise counsel, predictions, and precognition of the future. An altomisayoq is the agency through which the gods contact people.

The moon was just past full and backlighted a blanket of low hanging clouds pearl white. The evening star was so huge and bright that only it, and the moon, was visible in the night sky. Approaching midnight, Sebastian and I were let off by a taxi in lower Cusco, near San Sebastian, a district drenched in the filth of poverty. There were no streetlights and the road was in such a state of disrepair as to be nothing more than rough dirt, loose stones, and huge holes. This was no place to linger. Sebastian immediately headed up a steep hill at a fast pace, and I trotted behind. The incline was extreme and jagged where part of the bank had eroded way leaving gaping holes leading to a steep drop off.

After an hour of breathlessness, the labor more intense due to the endless obstacles in our way: barking mangy dogs, crumbling steps, gnarled hillside pocked with potholes and discarded adobe blocks that gave the impression that the world was coming to an end, we arrived at a cluster of huts and sheds perched precariously on the top of the farthest hill. These broken down shambles, all the more ominous because of the dark, were beyond belief. Ragged dogs darted in the shadows of the moon and clouds. A scrawny cat too famished to hunt for rats, eyed us from under a pile of rotting boards. It was as if the inhabitants had abandoned all sense of personal value and simply existed in whatever manner possible.

Unbelievably, this was the residence of Doña Maria, the elder of two remaining Q'ero altomisayoqs, and considered the greatest living shaman, an oracle of power. Her middle-aged son, Manuel, showed us to a tiny room with a dirt floor and one tiny opening for a window. After a long, silent wait, the altomisayoq arrived.

At least eighty, but spry and flexible, the diminutive Doña Maria took her place on the earthen floor atop a pile of alpaca furs. A single candle lighted the space, empty except for a bench and furs, more a stable than a room. Sebastian and I sat on the plain plank bench, squeezed together side by side. Manual sat on a miniature stool, and his wife positioned opposite us sat crossed-legged on the earthen floor.

Sebastian introduced me as "doctor Santiago," here to speak with Apu Ausangate. An altomisayoq holds the power to directly summon the great Apu, who speaks in ancient Quechua. In this way, one holds consul with the invisible. I brought all the appropriate gifts and offerings: tobacco, raisins, wine, cane alcohol, coca, and Peruvian Soles. Sebastian started by gifting every one coca leaves, and we began the customary process of offering k'intus to each other.

They conversed in Quechua among themselves, and I picked up

phrases here and there: "Santiago is one among us who understands the way of the Q'ero, who has suffered in his own skin the hardships of the sierra, who has been to Ausangate, who is a traditional misa carrier, who has encountered the spirits of the forest, yakumama and sachamama."

"Hai, hai." Manual says softly.

I was silent, respectful. Taking a handful of mapacho cigarettes, I offer them to Doña Maria. The oracle immediately put one to her lips and Sebastian quickly produced a match to light it for her. I passed more around and we smoked one after the other until they were gone. In between smokes, Manuel poured thimble-sized amounts of canasa, pure sugar cane alcohol. It bite my tongue, but warmed me inside. After that we sipped sugary red wine, which I also brought. "Salute! Salute!" Upon downing the strong brew, we smoked more, talked more, chewed more coca leaves, and snacked on raisins that I'd bought at the market in Cusco.

Then, on her uncuño a top a fresh pile of coca leaves, I placed a fist full of huayruru, red and white carnations, and a one hundred Peruvian Sol bill. The mapachos and canasa gone, she repositioned herself and we began. Manuel snuffed out the candle and we covered our heads and shoulders with shawls and blankets. It was pitch black and in the thin air, a thousand feet higher than Cusco, I was suffocating. Quiet. No one stirred.

Out of the absolute silence came a shrill, animated voice, Doña Maria's personal Apu, and ancient ally of absolute power. After a while, there was a pause, silence and darkness, and then a raspy, masculine voice boomed from all directions. Apu Ausangate.

Sebastian spoke for me, "Papito," he respectfully addressed the Apu in a gentle, almost kindly voice. Lost in the haze of coca, tobacco, and alcohol, I could not follow every thing he said. I huddled under my poncho. Sounds of wings and feathers filled the room. In twenty minutes, it was over.

Manuel lit the candle and in broken Spanish offered this translation: "Ausangate is pleased with your work. All is well and your path is open. But you and Sebastian must return again to the mountain. This time you will go directly to Apu Suryamana. Is that clear? Do you have any questions, Santiago?"

I was taken aback...only Sebastian knows of the man from my dream, in Cusco, and of our experiences on the mountain in 2008. I asked about Suryamana.

"Yes, Suryamana is real. This Apu stands between Apus Kallangate and Collquecruz," Manuel answered.

Then I described the important parts of my dream and my encounter on the mountain. There was no doubt that they accepted my dream and visions as actual events. There was no hesitation in their tone of voice.

"Santiago, when the time is right, as soon as possible upon your return next year, we will return to Ausangate. This time we journey straight to Apu Suryamana. You will ascend alone to summon the mountain spirit to become your personal Apu." Sebastian told me.

Doña Maria agreed. "Tell him the rest," she urged.

"You need to know that there are three types of work on the path of Ayni," Sebastian began: "There is every day Ayni, the equal exchange of goods or labor. We have spoken much about this already. The second form is *aynillank'ay*. This is when one person provides for many. Others come to help because it is an honor to serve such a person. There is no expectation of payment or compensation. And, there is a third type, *aynimita*. This is global Ayni. One's reason for being is to exist for Ayni, to live in Ayni, to express munay in the world."

"All is good." Doña Maria said. "Santiago, you are just starting. Journey with the blessing of Apu Ausangate."

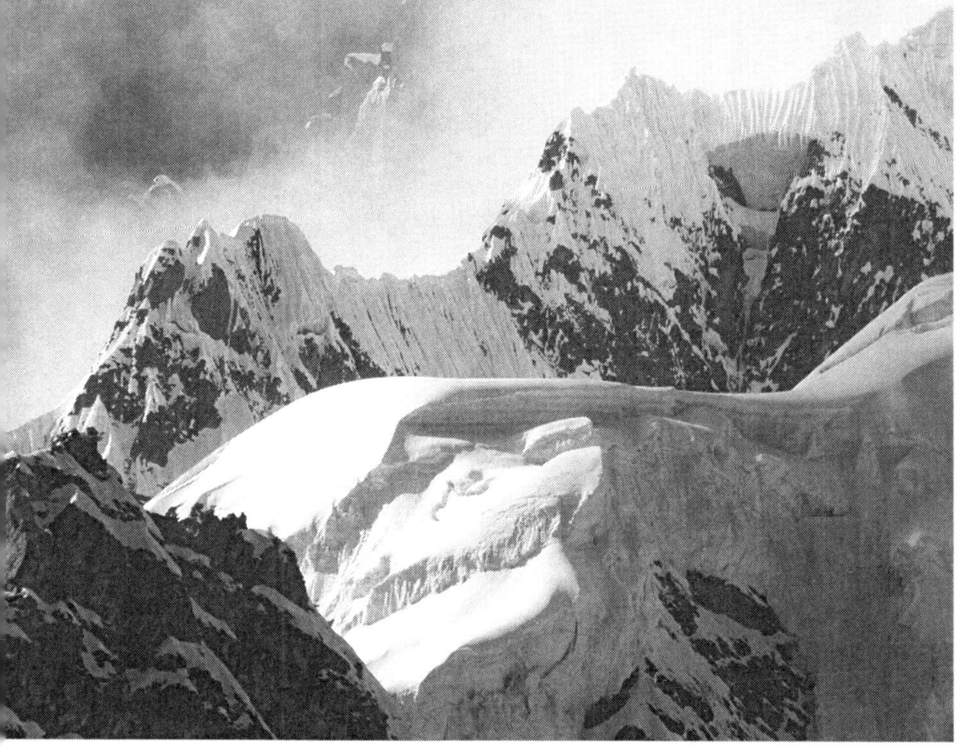

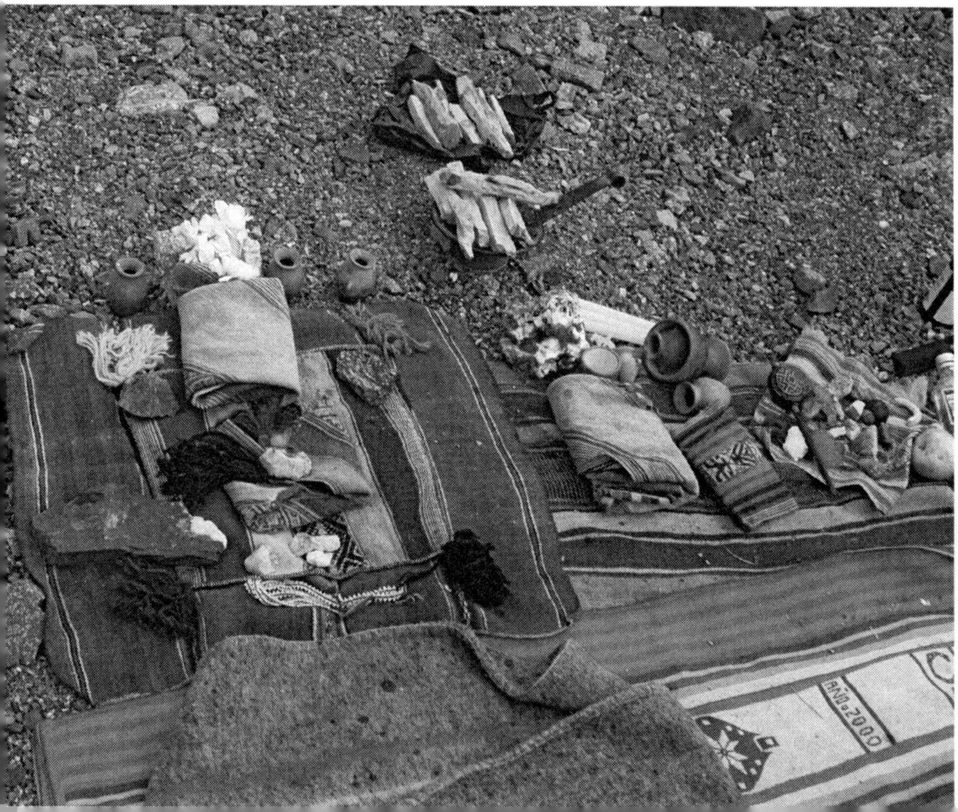
AÑO 2000

Previous page:

Above: Snow ridges in front of Ausangate peak.

Below: Santiago's misa (left) next to Sebastian's misa.

~ Sebastian's ~
NOTE

Ausangate is the oldest mountain in Tahuantinsuyu. To us, the name means, "master teacher." I want the world to know about the Apu and to learn about Ayni. It is not enough to go to the mountain. We must learn their connection to all things in the body of Pachamama. Every thing in human life and nature is related, that is why we say "all my relations," all living things including sacred stones and Apus, lakes and rivers, mountains and forests are part of us. We are part of them.

Santiago's personal connection with Apu Ausangate and his guardian Apu Suryamana, make his work important. The Apus speak through our sacred stones. They are portals of energy that carry the message of the Apus. Santiago speaks for them. This message is important for everyone. We all need to learn the way of Ayni. That is why we are offering it to everyone with a good heart, who are called by the Apus, who love Pachamama, to take the *aynikarpay,* to become *aynipampamisayoq,* to be one who lives and teaches Ayni to everyone in the world.

~ QUESTIONS FOR ~
# FURTHER DISCUSSION

1. In what way is *Anyi* comparable to the "Golden Rule?"
2. Can traditional indigenous cultures and their wisdom keepers transmit ancestral knowledge into useful teachings for our times?
3. What differences between imagination and reality occur to Santiago in the story?
4. What role does synchronicity play in Santiago's encounters with Sebastian? Does it imply non-ordinary reality?
5. How does lucid dreaming cross over into waking reality? Waking reality into the dreamtime?
6. Why do the Q'ero make no distinction between dream, vision, and their sense of reality?
7. How do Santiago's experiences of non-ordinary reality compare to the teachings of other indigenous shamans?
8. Is the teaching of Suryama apocryphal?
9. Why does Sebastian accept Santiago as a rightful member of his family group?
10. Why do we not have more teachers like Sebastian and Santiago in Western culture?

~ Notes & ~
REFERENCES

1. *Diccionario Quechua Espanol Quechua,* Municipalidad del Qospo, Kuipata, Qosqo (Cusco), Peru, 1995. Originally founded in 1953, the institute gained government approval in 1990 resulting in a Quechua language academy in Cusco, and is dedicated to maintaining the purity of the Quechua language. It holds that the Quechua spoken in Cusco, since it was the Inkan capital, should be the official standard for all Quechua in Peru, if not in all Andean countries where Quechua is spoken. The academy promotes the Quechua alphabet established by the Peruvian government in 1975, which corresponds to the alphabet used in this dictionary first printed in 1995.

2. *The Andean Codex* was originally published by Hampton Roads Publishing Company in 2005, and is now with Red Wheel/Weiser/Conari Publishers. Newburyport, MA.

3. *Zenaido meloda*

4. Vicuñas *(Vicugna vicugna)* are native to the high alpine areas of the Andes. They are the wild relative of llamas and alpacas. Vicuñas produce small amounts of extremely fine wool, which is very expensive because each animal can only be shorn every three years. Pieces of vicuña wool, a natural auburn rust color, are used in Q'ero ceremonies of reciprocity to form the first offering for a despacho.

5. Pachacamac is the contemporary spelling for the archeological

site south of Lima. *Pachakamaq* is the Quechua spelling for the creator of the universe. They are pronounced the same.

6. *Erythroxylum coca*

7. Hillman, James, *The Dream and the Underworld*. 1979, New York: William Morrow Paperbacks.

8. *Cantua buxifolila*

9. In comparison, Huascarán, the highest mountain in Peru, is 22,205 feet. The highest in the Andes is Aconcagua in Argentina at 22,834 feet. Mt. McKinley, the highest peak in North America is 20,320 feet. And, Mt. Everest, the highest mountain in the world, is 29,035 feet.

10. *Vicugna pacos*

11. *Llama glama*

12. *Vicugna vicugna*

13. Ch'uño is a freeze-dried potato product traditionally made by Quechua and Aymara communities of Peru and Bolivia.

14. *Giardia lamblia*

15. *Vanellus resplendens*

16. *Bruserea graveolens*

17. *Nicotiana tabacum*

18. Laszlo, Ervin, *Science and the Akashic Field*. 2004, Rochester, Vermont: Inner Traditions.

19. Loori, John Daido, *The True Dharma Eye: Zen Master Dogen's Three Hundred Koans* 2009, Boston, MA: Shambhala. Zen Master Eihei Dogen (1200-1253) was the monk, poet, thinker, essayist, and visionary who brought Chinese Zen to Japan, where it became Soto Zen. His work is among the most extensively studied Buddhist writings in the Western world. His literary style was to state something, then, Zen-like, contradict it with another statement. Therefore, he is best understood, not in context, but in the expansiveness of his teaching, catching glimpses of

enlightenment below the surface of the discursive mind.

20. Hausman, Gerald, *Tunkashila* 2011, Santa Fe, NM: Speaking Volumes. A simple stone, a chip off the holy mountain, like the prized sacred stones of a Q'ero shaman, speaks the ancestral language and is the best storyteller of the creation of all things, according to the mountain.

21. Han Shan, *Cold Mountain Poems: Zen Poems of Han Shan, Shih Te, and Wang Fan-chih* 2009, Boston, MA: Shambhala. The recluse monk who called himself Han Shan ("Cold Mountain") lived in a cave in the secluded Tiantai Mountains in Chekiang Province, China. It is believed he lived in the eight century, but his true identity and life story remain a mystery.

22. Han Shan, *Han Shan, The Cold Mountain Poems.* Gary Synder translation: http://www.hermetica.info/hanshan.htm.

23. *Vultur gryphus*

24. *Ormosia cocinea*

Glossary of
QUECHUA TERMS

Acllahuasi (Akllawasi): temple complex for reclusive women initiates.

Ajii ("ah-hee"): a capsicum chili family native to Peru and extremely hot.

Ajutas: Andean sandals.

Allin: good, excellent.

Altomisayoq: the highest level of Andean shaman-priests, one who connects directly with the Apus.

Amaru: serpent, Inkan symbol of wisdom.

Amauta: a sage, wise one, one of awakened consciousness

Anka: hawk or eagle.

Antisuyu: the eastern part of the Inkan Empire.

Apu: the tutelary spirit that resides in the snow-covered mountain peaks.

Apukuna: (Apus in Spanish and English) plural of Apu

Aqha *(chicha* in Spanish): a fermented beverage made from sprouted corn and used as staple in the Andes.

Aqhamama: ancient Quechua name for Cusco (Qosqo)

Awki ("auw-key"): nature spirits that reside in and protect mountains, caves, springs, trees, and rocks formations. The soul of a natural place.

Awkikuna: plural of Awki.

Ayahuasca (Ayawaskha, "aya-waz-ka"): the entheogenic liquid medicine made by slowly brewing pieces of the ayahuasca vine *(Banisteropsis caapi)* with chakruna leaves *(Pysichotria viridis)*.

Ayni: the principle of reciprocity central to Andean spiritual practice and daily life.

Aynikawsay: Ayni in daily life.

Aynimisaq'epe: the first sacred bundle in Q'ero shamanism.

Aynimunaykawsay: to be in the state of munay, love and beauty, through Ayni.

Capac: one greater than leader.

Chakana: Andean cross.

Capacunna: emperor.

Ch'aska: the most brilliant star.

Ch'ulhu: multicolored knitted Andean cap.

Ch'uñu: freeze dried dehydrated potato.

Ch'uspa: small, rectangular, tightly woven bags used to carry coca leaves.

Chakra: agricultural fields for plantings.

Chinchaysuyu: the northern region of the Inkan Empire.

Chiri: cold.

Chiri Chiri: very cold.

Choqlo: an ear of corn.

Chuku: a brimmed hat.

Collasuyu: the southern region of the Inkan Empire.

Cuntisuyu: the western region of the Inkan Empire.

Haiwariquy: specific offering to an Apu.

Haku: to get going. Hakuchis: let's go.

Hanan: upper part.

Hananpacha: the upper world of spiritual beings according to Andean cosmology.

Hanpi: medicine.

Hanpiq: healer

Hanpiqipu: misa dedicated to healing.

Hanpiy: invoking curative energy

Hanpuy: come

Hatun: large, big.

Hillap'a or Illap'a: lightning.

Huaca (Waka): a sacred natural setting or burial site, or shrine along a seq'e line.

Huachuma: *Echinopsis pachanoi,* San Pedro cactus.

Huancamayoq: a specialist in performing ritual offerings and tending huacas.

Huayruru (Wayruru): *Ormosia coccinea,* red and black seeds made into necklaces and bracelets and used as love charms and protection against bad luck.

Illa Tesqi Wiraqocha: Creator of the universe, Supreme Being.

Inka (Inca): Emperor, monarch.

Inkari: the title of the return of the Inka.

Inti: the physical sun and the spiritual presence inherent in the sun's life giving energy.

Intikhana: a being of light, limitless and at one with Inti.

K'intu: three coca leaves symbolizing the three worlds of Andean cosmology and the three ethical and moral principles of the Andean way.

Glossary of Quechua Terms

Kallpa ("kai-pa"): the life force, energy, vigor.

Kamaq: creator.

Karpay: a special ceremony involving numerous shamans at which time initiations and titles may be conferred.

Kawsay: life.

Kawsaypacha: the world of living energy.

Kay: to exist, to live, to be.

Kaypacha: the middle dimension of Andean cosmology and the world of matter in which we live, the world of daily affairs.

Killa: moon. Mamakilla, "mother moon" is the spirit of the moon.

Kuka: *Erythroxylum coca,* the coca plant and leaves.

Kukak'intu: three perfectly shaped coca leaves used as an act of Ayni to the Apus.

Kukamukllu: coca seeds.

Kukawatoq or Kukaqhawaq: person who divines with coca leaves.

Kukawayaka: ceremonial coca leaf bag.

Kuntisuyu: western region of Tawantinsuyu.

Kuntur: the condor.

Kurakakullek: the highest level of Andean shamanic initiation.

Llank'ay: ("yan-kay") physical labor, work, the attitude of service to others rendered with love in the spirit of Ayni.

Llikla: *(manta* in Spanish), colorful shawl used as a ceremonial cloth to form the misaq'epe.

Llipht'a: alkaline paste made from cacao or quinoa ash and lime chewed with coca leaves to extract the active alkaloids.

Mamaq'epe: the "mother" sacred bundle used during initiations.

Mayu: the Milky Way and a central aspect of Inkan cosmology.

Misa or Misal: A shaman's sacred objects used to connect with the

Awkikuna and Apukuna, and typically wrapped in a ritual cloth, the misaq'epe.

Misaq'epe: ceremonial bundle containing the shaman's sacred objects.

Misaqollu: decorative stones and objects used to adorn the misa.

Misarumi: sacred stones given by an Apu.

Munay: loving-kindness, one of the three Andean ethical and moral principles.

Munaycha: beautiful.

Orcopuntakarpay: initiation to form a personal relationship with an Apu.

Pacha: the wholeness of life in space-time.

Pachakamacha: human social life.

Pachakamaq: creator of the universe.

Pachakawsay: lifespan.

Pachakuti: the ninth Inka, and the time between eras when the world is shaken and transformed.

Pachamama: the earth mother in space-time.

Pampamisayoq: Andean shaman-priest who is a specialist in ritual sacred worship and healing.

Papa: potato.

Papawatya: roasted potato.

Papawayk'u: boiled potato.

Pakuq (Paqo): an Andean shaman-priest.

Phuku: to blow.

Phukuyr'tti: ritual blowing usually on coca leaves, also used for healing or directed towards the east as a symbolic act of offering the life force within one self to the rising sun.

Phuquchu: Fur bag made of baby alpaca used to summon the Apus.

Pumarunas: Inkan priests dedicated to ceremonies associated with the puma and important in festivals related to Cuzco, the city of the puma.

Punchu: poncho.

Q'epe: carrying bundle

Q'ente: hummingbird.

Qhaqya: thunder.

Qocha: lake.

Qochamama or mamaqocha: "mother" lake, the sea.

Quipu or Khipu: an assemblage of cotton and alpaca threads woven and knotted that constituted a tactile system of mathematics and information transmission.

Qoyllur Rit'i: site of the largest annual festival in the Andes.

Quipucamayoqs: specialists in reading quipus.

Riti: snow.

Runa: person.

Runasimi: Quechua, the people's language.

Seq'e ("sec-keys") or ceques: the system of lines and corresponding shrines radiating out of Cuzco.

Sumaq: wonderful, delicious.

Suyus: the four regions of the Inkan empire, the four cardinal directions.

Tahuantinsuyu (Tawantinsuyu): the "four corners of the world" signifying the Inkan empire.

Ukhupacha: the interior or lower world of Andean cosmology.

Uncuño: special woven clothes for coca leaves and used as part of the ceremonial misa.

Unku: the pre-Hispanic black tunic still worn by traditional Q'ero under their poncho.

Uño: water.

Uramama: "mother" coca.

Watya: method of baking underground.

Willaq Uma: Inkan solar priest, a fully integrated human being, one in direct contact with the Apus and at one with the natural environment and spiritual worlds.

Wiraqocha: gentleman.

Yachay: the superior consciousness we arrive at through love and work.

Yanatin: a divine pair of mountains or other sacred natural formations.

~ About ~
THE AUTHOR

Dr. J. E. Williams is the author of *The Andean Codex,* three works on integrative medicine, and one book of poetry. He has written about Earth-based teachings and sustainable medicine in Shaman's Drum, Herbal Gram, Sacred Hoop, Body and Soul, and other new thought publications and integrative medical journals. Since 1967, he has lived and worked with indigenous tribes to protect and preserve culture, environment, and intellectual rights. He is the founder of AyniGLOBAL, a non-profit organization dedicated to principle-guided living, and personal and planetary change.

~ About ~
AYNIGLOBAL

AyniGLOBAL is a 501(c)(3) non-profit organization established in Washington, D.C, in 2010 with the approval of Sebastian's branch of traditional Q'ero.

Mission: To protect and preserve traditional indigenous cultures and ancestral lands including people, animals, plants and water systems.

Purpose: To have maximum impact in the following areas:

- Social justice for indigenous people including legal assistance and community mediation with qualified experts.

- Indigenous health and medicine including ethnobotanical and community health research.

- Education including early childhood education and adult learning.

- Biodiversity protection including preservation of traditional homeland integrity to ensure ecosystem stability that will endure for generations.

- Cooperation with indigenous wisdom keepers for the dissemination of native principles related to ethics and environmental issues to be presented to world leaders, as well as in partnerships with governmental and non-governmental agencies, and strategic affiliations with local communities, educational institutions, businesses, corporations, and non-profit organizations.

ayniglobal

For more information visit:
www.ayniglobal.org